KEEP THE MEMORIES,
LOSE THE STUFF

KEEP THE MEMORIES, LOSE THE STUFF

Declutter, Downsize, and
Move Forward with Your Life

MATT PAXTON

with Jordan Michael Smith

PORTFOLIO • PENGUIN

Portfolio / Penguin
An imprint of Penguin Random House LLC
penguinrandomhouse.com

AARP

Most Portfolio books are available at a discount when purchased in quantity for sales promotions or corporate use. Special editions, which include personalized covers, excerpts, and corporate imprints, can be created when purchased in large quantities. For more information, please call (212) 572-2232 or e-mail specialmarkets@penguinrandomhouse.com. Your local bookstore can also assist with discounted bulk purchases using the Penguin Random House corporate Business-to-Business program. For assistance in locating a participating retailer, e-mail B2B@penguinrandomhouse.com.

Library of Congress Cataloging-in-Publication Data
Names: Paxton, Matt, author. | Smith, Jordan Michael, author.
Title: Keep the memories, lose the stuff : declutter, downsize, and move forward with your life / Matt Paxton ; with Jordan Michael Smith.
Description: [New York, New York] : Portfolio/Penguin, [2022] | Includes bibliographical references and index.
Identifiers: LCCN 2021047797 (print) | LCCN 2021047798 (ebook) | ISBN 9780593418970 (paperback) | ISBN 9780593418987 (ebook)
Subjects: LCSH: Storage in the home. | Orderliness. | Self-management (Psychology) | House cleaning. | Conduct of life.
Classification: LCC TX324.5 .P39 2022 (print) | LCC TX324.5 (ebook) | DDC 648/.8—dc23/eng/20211202
LC record available at https://lccn.loc.gov/2021047797
LC ebook record available at https://lccn.loc.gov/2021047798

Printed in the United States of America
2nd Printing

BOOK DESIGN BY ELLEN CIPRIANO

A range of AARP print and e-books are available at AARP's online bookstore, aarp.org/bookstore, and through local and online bookstores.

To Zoë,
my muse, my mentor in simplicity,
and my person.
Thank you for teaching me
that less is more.

CONTENTS

KEEP THE MEMORIES,
LOSE THE STUFF

INTRODUCTION

Why You Can't Let Go

I HAVE SEEN IT ALL.

I've met a couple whose unimaginably creepy collection of over a hundred dolls put them at risk of eviction. I've met a woman who hoarded her chickens and all their eggs—even the bad ones—inside her house because she couldn't part with them. As a decluttering and organizing expert with over twenty years of experience, I've met countless people who let clutter rule their lives—and I have helped nearly all of them let go of their stuff and start living.

From being the featured cleaner on *Hoarders* and hosting *Legacy List with Matt Paxton* to giving a TED Talk on extreme cleaning and helping Jimmy Kimmel clean out an office, I am known as the guy who gets knee deep in stuff for a living to help people declutter and downsize. I have helped thousands of people from all walks of life, of all ages and income levels, leave behind belongings that no longer serve them so that they can finally take the next step.

So how was it that, just a year ago, I found myself paralyzed with fear at the prospect of downsizing and moving my own stuff?

It was the summer of 2020. COVID-19 cases were spiking and I'd been quarantined at my home in Richmond, Virginia, for a few months. As someone who thrives around people, I had gotten a bit stir crazy. What's more, I was *in love*.

For more than a year, I'd been dating a woman named Zoë, who I was bonkers about. She is funny, smart, kind, everything a man could want. But she lived in Georgia and one of her four kids was in high school, so moving was not an option for her. For us be together, I had to make the decision to move.

If I was going to move, I desperately needed to declutter and downsize. I mean, I have three kids. For all my years of exposure to the problems created by excess—keep in mind that one of my clients held on to a cherished jar of mackerel for thirty-seven years—I hadn't stopped myself from accumulating a dizzying amount of stuff. My kids had enough Legos to build us a new house. I had enough tools to build Noah's Ark several times over. There were superfluous pieces of every type of furniture imaginable, from beds to desks to couches.

Let's be honest here: The chances of me getting a woman like Zoë are slim. This was my golden ticket to romantic happiness, and I knew it. But I felt immobilized in the face of the distress and pain of moving. I couldn't bring myself to part with all the heirlooms I cherished.

To start, there was Dad's art—about fifty paintings strewn about the house. He'd passed away twenty years earlier, and his art kept his memory alive in my house. Then there were my poker chips. A former gambling devotee, I'd collected dozens of $5 and $1 chips. As an entrepreneur, I'd accumulated hundreds of books. Parting with them felt like abandoning the ideas that helped me make my livelihood.

I had lived in my home for only ten years. A good chunk of time, sure, but some of my clients have been in their homes for forty or even fifty years. They have lived entire lifetimes in their one spot—and I have helped them move on from it, with all the difficulty that change carries. And here I was, panicking at the thought of leaving behind a decade's worth of belongings.

As I thought through my decision to move, I realized that my anxieties were rooted in more than just material things. I'd been living in Richmond for most of my life, and leaving it all for faraway Georgia seemed scary. Who am I if not a Virginian? The year I was born, my grandfather bought four season tickets to the local college basketball team—my beloved Richmond Spiders, surely the greatest team in sports history. Just over forty years later, my three sons sat in those same seats with me, watching the same team I'd watched with my grandfather decades earlier. The prospect of moving brought my identity into question.

Then there was what I call the paralysis of *what-iffing*: What if I didn't like Georgia? I'd never lived there, or anywhere outside Richmond for any length of time. What if I missed Virginia—or, worse, lost touch with my friends and neighbors? What if I went through the anguish and exertion of moving, only to realize that I'd made a mistake? All my business contacts were in my hometown—I couldn't be sure I'd find new business once I moved. And of course, there was the matter of my kids. What if they didn't make new friends? What if they hated their new home? This fear of change made me feel like I'd never reach a decision.

I became so intimidated by the task of sorting, packing, and moving that I seriously considered calling off my plans—

even though that would mean breaking up with the woman of my dreams. I called Zoë and told her I didn't know if I could do it, that it was simply too stressful. And Zoë—a devout minimalist—understood but was frustrated that my stuff was stopping us from building a life together.

I was miserable. For two weeks, I moped around the house, looking even more unkempt and disheveled than normal. My laundry piled up, and for the first time ever, so did the dishes in my sink. I ate way too much mint chocolate chip ice cream, straight from the tub. One night I watched *The Notebook* and *La La Land* back-to-back, feeling sorry for myself and wondering if I'd ever find love again.

Finally, after two weeks, my ex-wife, the mother of my three boys, called and said she wanted to move to Georgia, too. She wanted a change in her life, and she knew that Zoë was perfect for me. Well, if she was moving to Georgia, then I had no excuse. My ex-wife—who, yes, is clearly a good person—forced my hand. She helped me realize that when I left my stuff in Virginia behind, I would still have the memories and the relationships. The discomfort would be temporary, and the payoff would be worth it. I called Zoë, told her the news, and began making plans to move while trying to deal with the pack of butterflies and pounds of knots in my stomach.

Man, am I glad I did it. More than glad—exhilarated. Relieved. Moving allowed me to open a whole new chapter in my life. It was a step that I needed to take for my own well-being, and that of my family. Zoë and I are now married, our combined seven kids (which is one more than the Brady Bunch, if you're keeping track) living under the same roof.

Maybe you picked up this book because you, like me, needed to make a big change that requires a big move. Maybe you're an older couple who needs to clean out your well-lived-in family home. Maybe you just have too much stuff and need to pare it down a little. Maybe you are part of a couple merging households. Maybe you're a caregiver helping a loved one transition to senior living. Maybe you have been left the task of decluttering after the death of a relative or friend.

In this book, I will reveal the time-tested, step-by-step system I have perfected over the last twenty-plus years of professionally helping people downsize, declutter, and move. Unlike almost all the other experts out there, I will not tell you to check your emotions at the door. I know that a set of china, a packed bookshelf, or a height chart hanging on the wall are never "just stuff." Instead, I will help you—or help you help someone else—discover which possessions are worth holding on to and which you can live without. Throughout this process, I will help you honor your memories, while letting go of (most of) your stuff.

. . .

People always ask me, "How in the world did you get into your line of business?" No one wakes up one day and decides they want to clean up hoarded homes for a living.

My introduction into the downsizing world came in 2001, when I was twenty-four years old, I sure needed *something* to find me . . .

After a few mediocre years studying business, I graduated (barely) from a college in Virginia and landed a job as an in-house analyst at Caesars Palace in Lake Tahoe. It was as wild as you can imagine, living on the seventh floor of the hotel. I won't sugarcoat it: Selfish and self-indulgent, I did what I wanted, when I wanted to do it, without caring about the consequences. Unsurprisingly, I was soon fired. Out of luck, out of funds, and out of options, I moved back to my dad's house in my hometown of Richmond. I was a wreck.

Dad and I had always been close, and we got even closer when my parents divorced when I was six. I lived with him in the city every other weekend. He was a fun-loving cowboy in the jungle. He fit in everywhere and nowhere, and he *loved* life every second he could.

So I was devastated when, a few months after I moved back home, Dad's doctor told him he had carcinoma, a cancerous tumor the size of a softball, and gave him six weeks at most to live. Six weeks! He was only fifty-two, but he lived at a pace that was unsustainable. Nobody was as shocked as I was by his diagnosis. Who imagines their superhero is mortal? Can you envision Superman dying? I was overwhelmed with sadness.

When he died, it became my responsibility to clean out his home.

Dad lived in a four-story, four-thousand-square-foot, hundred-year-old brick row house. And over his final months, the last thing on his mind was decluttering. Instead of mourning the impending end of his life and cleaning out his stuff, he did the only thing he knew how to do, the thing he did best, the thing he loved most: He threw parties. He set up camp on the porch, where he'd spent so much time entertaining over the years, and people came by to pay their respects. Richmond is a pretty big city with a small-town feel, and it seemed like everyone visited the porch to say goodbye. People sat with my dad as he quickly deteriorated. But here's what surprised me: Dad's spirit stayed vibrant even as his body failed. He and his friends—there were a lot of them—told stories and laughed. They swapped memories and they joked. I began to clue into something: *Stories would be a way for us all to keep my father alive after he died.* That lesson, on the eternal life that storytelling uniquely offers, was the first spark in what eventually became my career.

When he died a few short months later, I didn't have a career; I just had a big hole in my heart and a massive house to go through. Because Dad died so swiftly, his house was left looking the same way it had always looked: full of life. Someone had to pick through all that stuff. Someone had to decide what to keep and what to get rid of—and where that stuff should go.

That someone was me. Thus, my work downsizing began.

Dad kept everything. The prospect of cleaning his house looked to me like that scene in *The Shawshank Redemption* where Tim Robbins's character, Andy Dufresne, crawls five hundred yards through a filthy sewer pipe, except I wasn't going to emerge outside of prison as a free man. The only thing attractive to me about cleaning the house was that it would delay my need to look for a "real" job.

My brother moved in to assist. Even my mom, who had divorced my dad twenty years earlier, helped out. And so what might have been a lonely, sad time turned into a family reunion.

We started sifting through the mountains of belongings. Dad had been an artist turned ad man, and we found his drawings, half-finished paintings, sketchbooks, and copies of every ad he'd ever created. Slowly I was discovering new sides to someone I thought I knew better than anyone in the world. My mother and I couldn't stop laughing when we went through his closet and found his imitation *Miami Vice* outfits from the 1980s: pink and blue T-shirts, a white blazer with super-tight sleeves at the end and shoulder pads. The funniest find was in a crumpled brown paper bag in one of the bedroom drawers. I opened it cautiously, expecting . . . well, I dunno. My heart beat faster. What I found was my father's ponytail. He knew I hated it and had saved it for me, knowing that I'd find it. My dying father had pranked me! I can hear him laugh as I write this story. That clipped ponytail encapsulated everything absurd and mischievous I loved about him. I feel blessed that I had the time to clean out his home and find it.

This is one benefit of cleaning out an estate, and it's often overlooked. Spending time with loved ones' possessions is a way to connect with them, even after they're gone. Those possessions can be deeply personal, comforting you through a difficult time. What is Winston Churchill without his cigar and top hat, or Audrey Hepburn without her Tiffany pearls and black dress? Indulge in your impulse to reminisce and reflect as you sift through the leftover items. This ordeal is a productive form of grieving—it can be an emotional experience, but also a healing one.

Cleaning out Dad's home required months of effort. I worked from 10 a.m. to 6 p.m. nearly every day. It took so long because there were fifty-two years of possessions in his house, but also because we took our time. We had *fun*. We savored the process rather than rushing it. We celebrated my father's funny, absurd life by recounting the stories behind his stuff to one another. That option—that simple attitude adjustment—is available to anyone charged with decluttering a space.

WHERE TO START

An entire life was in my father's house. We had hard choices to make about Dad's belongings. Everything there was his, so everything reminded us of him. But obviously we couldn't keep everything. For one thing, I knew I'd soon be moving out of that house and into a one-bedroom apartment just bigger than a shoebox. No space for clutter there. Second, I didn't actually *want* to keep everything—I just couldn't stand the thought of getting rid of my father's stuff.

We had to, though. And since you're reading this book, you're probably facing the same dilemma—whether it's your own or a loved one's stuff.

When I was tasked with clearing out my Dad's home, I started first by going through and deciding what I wanted to keep. Dad always liked jewelry. Short of keeping his underwear (I didn't do that, but you wouldn't believe the things I've seen people keep), wearing his ring was one of the ways I could keep him close to me. I also held on to my father's bow ties, cuff links, original artwork, and some vintage Hawaiian shirts.

I didn't realize it then, but I was beginning to develop a concept that's central to my work today: a *Legacy List*. At its core, a Legacy List is a method of narrowing down the essential items in your life. Whether you're trying to declutter, downsize, or move, putting together a Legacy List can help you make the most difficult choices about what to do with objects that you feel overwhelmed by—and that are important enough to keep. It's like a skeleton key that can help you open a door to a better life. That's what I teach you in this book.

There's a reason, though, that I don't start with the Legacy List. It's not the first part of the decluttering process. Back when I was starting out, I didn't know that, of course. I just knew that my father had died and I wanted to get dibs on whatever prize possessions I could fit into my small apartment.

DECLUTTERING IN ORDER

When my dad died, I had no guidance on how to go about decluttering. I just did whatever came to my mind or tackled what was in front of me. Now that I know better, I have an order I recommend to clients, which you'll see unfold throughout the rest of this book:

- **Uncover the stories behind the clutter.** This is by far the most crucial step that creates a pathway for all the others. It's the step many other experts miss. You will learn how to find a receptive listener—or how to become one for someone else—and build the trust necessary to accept or give help.
- **Define your finish line.** You will learn how to identify—or help someone else identify—what you want your life to look like after you declutter, whether it's moving across the country, downsizing to a senior living community next door, or simply paring down the items in your existing home.

- **Take the first baby steps.** You will learn my most handy tips and tricks for digging in, including setting a deadline and doing what I call the "Ten-Minute Sweep."
- **Sort through pictures and documents.** Newspapers, magazines, books, and junk mail often contribute to clutter, and I help you quickly go through them. Photos and files of papers can be the most emotionally significant items in your home. You will learn how to scrutinize every paper and scrapbook without losing your patience—or losing that one valuable document in a stack of stuff!
- **Decide what to keep and build your Legacy List.** Choosing what to hold on to and what to get rid of will probably be the hardest part of decluttering. That's why it's such an important step in the process—once you complete it, you've already finished the toughest tasks. In addition, you'll have to know what you're keeping before you can move on to the next steps, which involve getting rid of stuff.
- **Decide what to give away.** You'll learn how to give your kids and other relatives what they want (which may be less than what you'd like to give them), sell valuables, donate to charity (and pick the right charity), and more.
- **Clean up.** Whether you're moving or staying, you'll want to thoroughly clean the place (unless, of course, you hire someone else to). You'll learn the secret tips I've collected

from cleaning houses for decades. You'll also find a list of invaluable supplies that will make this step easier. You'd be surprised how much more stuff reveals itself during this step, and how many more decisions you'll have to make.

- **Move forward.** You will learn the do's and don'ts of moving.

. . . .

Uncover the Stories Behind the Stuff

DID CLEANING OUT DAD'S SPACE spark an epiphany that decluttering is my lifelong purpose? Not at all. I was just happy to put off my job search for a few months while I figured things out. I still had no idea how I was going to earn a living. My father, my hero, was gone, and I was lost and wandering—and the only thing worse than being lost in life is being lost in life *and* broke.

I had one thing going for me, though: a community. People knew my grandfather, they knew my father, and now they knew me. I had my people. The upside of a tightly knit community is that people look out for you when you're down on your luck. The downside is that everyone knows the details of your life. Both realities played into what happened next.

Word got around that I had cleared out my dad's house and that I was looking for work. At church one Sunday, a kindly eighty-year-old woman—we'll call her Etta—came over to me. I'd known her my entire life—she and her loving squad of bridge players, with their immaculate, blue-tinted white hair. No matter what was going on in their lives, these women got their hair done at the beauty parlor every other Thursday afternoon.

Etta told me she'd heard I was looking for some ways to make money and offered to help me out. She lived in an old colonial house like my father's, and her friends were encouraging her to downsize now that her beloved husband, Jim, had died. She was years away from going into senior living, she hastened to inform me. But she figured I could use some extra money. She asked if I could do some work for her.

I quickly agreed, happy to help her out and earn some cash. A few days later, I arrived at her home ready to clear out what I assumed were a few boxes.

Then I stepped inside. Etta's home was a sign of a well-lived life. Dishes and crystal of every type imaginable were stacked in her kitchen and dining room. Cases of wine and shelves of wineglasses. Linen tablecloths and napkins folded neatly. At least ten card tables and dozens of decks of cards. It looked to me like her home held enough to supply a banquet hall.

I had thought, going over to Etta's home, that helping her declutter would be depressing. Weren't we going to throw away a lifetime of stuff, after all? Wouldn't helping her clean out be like helping her write her own obituary?

That wasn't what happened at all. Over the next few weeks, Etta and I took pleasure in her favorite life stories. We didn't bury her best years; we celebrated them. She had an eager audience in me, and she was in control of how the organizational process worked. She took her time. Etta's memories were given another life when she recalled them to me—and in this chapter I'm giving them another life by recalling them to you. This is the most important part of the process—the part most experts miss entirely. If we don't know the stories behind the stuff, we will never be able to freely let go of it.

If you are in the process of decluttering, downsizing, or moving, telling your stories to an interested audience is the magic key. And if you're helping someone else, it's your responsibility to listen. In this chapter, I'm going to show you how to both tell and listen to the tales.

WHY DIFFERENT GENERATIONS COLLECT DIFFERENT STUFF

If you're cleaning out the home of older generations, you'll likely notice how differently they consumed and collected stuff than we do in our current era. I hadn't realized this until cleaning Etta's home. Etta was an entirely different species from me or my dad. As we talked that day, I understood for the first time the significance of that generation gap.

Etta was a child of the Great Depression. Those of us who have grown up in more prosperous times might not understand what it was like to come of age when scarcity was the norm, not the exception. But those who lived through it never forget it. Soup kitchens and bread lines. Labor strikes and Dust Bowls. "One-third of a nation ill-housed, ill-clad, and ill-nourished," as President Franklin Roosevelt said in 1937. These traumatic memories became part of a generation's DNA. Starting with Etta and continuing for the last twenty-plus years, I have worked with that generation and witnessed the indelible imprint the Depression left upon millions of people. It's not always detectable in their words or actions out in public—but it's visible in their homes.

But I didn't know that yet. So at first, I wondered why Etta seemed to keep everything. Why hold on to those skinny yellow plastic bags tossed on her porch every morning with the newspapers? And the rubber bands wrapped around the armrest of her rocking chair? She had a stack of bulletins from every church service I think she ever attended; it looked like fifty years of neatly stacked Sundays. I was stupefied at the sheer amount of *stuff* this petite woman possessed.

Starting in the dining room and moving to the basement and the attic, we went to work, packing things up, picking and choosing what to keep and what to donate or discard, and, most of all, talking and laughing.

And crying. Tears welled up in Etta's eyes as she looked at a note from her father, in his rough handwriting, when he'd left home for months to go out in the world in search of work. She showed me his pocket watch, which she remembered him pulling out of a vest pocket often to ensure they'd be on time for appointments. That story led to others: She and her brother splitting a single slice of bread because that was all they had to eat that day. The Christmas when all her mother could afford for her children was a gift of a single orange and a peppermint stick. Etta told me with delight, with gratitude for her good fortune, the luxurious treat of sucking the juice out of the orange through the peppermint stick.

I felt like I was not just helping Etta go through her stuff; I was in the trenches with her. As I got to know her, I began to understand why she had so much stuff: For people who had nothing at one time, anything they have is precious. More than sixty years later, Etta hadn't lost the feeling that one day, abundance might suddenly disappear, leaving her with nothing once again. And then every plastic bag, every last rubber band would be as precious as coins and paper bills.

Wading through her belongings and talking to Etta about her memories of deprivation, I started to understand something that would later become essential to my life's work: People hoard to cover up pain. The scarcity Etta had suffered when she was younger stayed with her for the rest of her life. She wanted to have enough in her home so that she would never, ever run out. And plastic bags and rubber bands aside, she was damned proud of the possessions she and Jim had worked their tails off to earn. That made parting with them all the more difficult.

Etta explained something else to me: As a full-time homemaker for decades, entertaining guests, friends, and family was deeply important to her. *That* was why she always kept the house spotless and stocked with enough supplies to serve a small army. When I first got there, I wondered: Who could ever use that many card tables? I'd been to some underground casinos in my time, but something told me that Etta wasn't a card shark running an after-hours club in her basement. And enough platters and serving utensils to open a catering business? Now I understood.

Jim had been a big-time tobacco executive. He was a strong, sturdy, reliable man—a pillar of the community. I admired him when I was young. People like him built Richmond into the city it is today. But now I was seeing Etta, too, as a pillar. For decades, even while raising two kids, she was ready at any time should Jim bring a colleague, supervisor, or client over to be fed and charmed. Her home, the items she took such pride in, proved her commitment to her family and community.

After I spent a few hours helping Etta sort through her memories, she began putting her stuff into perspective. This early in the process, we are only slowly coming around to the idea that it's not always the pocket watch we love; it's the person who wore it. The goal is not to make any hasty decisions about what to toss and what to keep. It's to begin to build the trust necessary to decide together. By the time Etta had recounted some of her most cherished memories, and I'd listened with an open mind and heart, she felt she trusted me enough for me to start doing my job.

HOW TO LISTEN WELL

Much of this book will outline the unmatchable worth of sharing stories. But the flip side of sharing stories is another vital practice: listening to them. To earn someone's confidence, you have to be fully present. Hour after hour, day after day. There are no shortcuts, and ideally there should be no multitasking. If you are helping people declutter, they might think you do not care about their stories, let alone want to hear about their past in great detail. Your job is to show that you care. Not just to say it, but to show it, which requires earning their trust along the way. And as I always remind my employees, the word "listen" has the same letters as the word "silent."

To listen intently, make sure you leave the technology in the car or at least in another room. I'm old school—I bring a pad of paper and a pen to take notes. I do not, under any circumstances, use an electronic device in front of clients. That includes cell phones, tablets, smart watches, and headphones with music. If I divert my attention every few minutes to check my email or look at an incoming text message, my clients sense my lack of interest. If you must have your device with you, put it on airplane mode and turn off the ringer and vibrator. Think how offensive it is if someone is pouring out his heart out to you and you respond by looking down at your buzzing watch. He now thinks something else is more important than he is, and is less inclined to trust you with his most treasured items as a result.

Be sure to make eye contact and to take mental notes of things to ask about when the person is done talking. Let him know you are writing down ideas or tasks to do later so you don't forget them. I often ask clients to hold on momentarily so I can write down all they are saying, and then I ask them to resume telling me the story. Most important, avoid talking about yourself. This isn't about you; it's about you listening. Don't keep trying to relate your life to his; this is a rare moment when it is 100 percent about him, so just listen and enjoy and be thankful that you are able to have this moment in time. You're helping him make major change in his life, and that's an immense privilege.

On one of the days I was working with Etta, while in her jam-packed attic, I picked up a grainy black-and-white picture of two young couples sitting at a table, smiling at the camera. The women, probably between eighteen and twenty years old, were simply beautiful. They wore pearls, white gloves, and fancy dresses. Both of the men were in military uniform, grinning, handsome, and happy.

"Who's this?" I asked.

Etta smiled. She pointed to one of the couples. "That's me and Jim."

"That's *you*?" I asked. Etta nodded. The woman standing in front of me was lovely and powerful, but she was a blue-haired eighty-year-old who looked a bit older. I, twenty-five years old and drunk with the delusions of eternal youthfulness, had a hard time squaring the photo with the woman before me.

"Etta," I said, "you were a knockout!" She smiled and then excitedly showed me a pack of matches that were nearly hidden amid the clutter. It bore the logo of a place named Tantilla Gardens. All my life I'd lived in Richmond, but I'd never even heard of Tantilla Gardens. Etta told me that the picture was taken there on the night her then-suitor Jim had just returned from World War II and got dropped off at the train station just up the street.

For Etta, *this* was the image that the photo brought to mind. For me, the snapshot was just a fading shot of two good-looking happy young couples. For Etta, the picture was a precious reminder of an unforgettable time in her life, an early glimpse of the man she'd spend her life with. It was proof of the world she'd once inhabited. Of the young man she'd once pined for, of the young woman she'd once been, and of the man she deeply loved for a lifetime. No wonder she had held on to it and to *everything* in her home. They were items that seemed random and unnecessary to me but contained life-affirming memories for her. She wasn't hoarding or holding on to junk; she was celebrating the incredible life that she and her husband had lived together. I was learning that this was more than just stuff. I was starting to realize in fact that it had almost nothing to do with the stuff; it was all about the memories behind the stuff.

She pointed out something in the photograph that I hadn't noticed: a paper bag sitting on the table. There was booze in it, she told me, giving me a mischievous look that made her appear for a moment as if she were eighteen years old all over again. Good Baptist ladies didn't drink in public, I knew—but if they did, they put the liquor bottle in a brown paper bag to be discreet.

"You must have had a *good* time," I said, winking at her.

"Oh, we did," she said, grinning. "I missed my parents' curfew that night."

Note that we didn't look at Etta's picture on the first day of our decluttering effort. It took some time before we spontaneously created that moment. This is another reason why you want to give yourself lots of time to do this work—so that you can relax and delve into the details of the items. I said earlier in this book that you want to jump into decluttering as soon as possible; don't wait until the last minute. On the other hand, you're going to take your time going through your stuff. This is more than just packing boxes and filling up trash bags. Just like writing a term paper in college, if you wait to cram all the work until the end, your grade will probably reflect that choice, and it will impact your permanent record. Decluttering should not be completed in one long weekend. Plan ahead for the time and people to properly help. Put it on the calendar. By knowing her eventual journey into senior living, Etta gave herself crucial preparatory time to enjoy the move calmly and confidently.

Etta and I talked about the night Jim had returned from the war safe and sound after being gone for so long. She cried remembering the moment captured in the item we held in our hands.

But talking to Etta about the photo, seeing the powerful emotions sweep over her as we reminisced, made me lose that image of the old blue-haired woman and see Etta as a full human being, whose life was filled with memories, experiences, and people she loved. In some ways, I realized, her attic, like the rest of her home, was a museum devoted to her long life.

Talking with Etta, I understood how she was so attached to what had initially seemed to me to be excessive amounts of plastic and glass. I can tell you a hundred stories about moving, but it won't seem weighty until you deal with your own stuff. It's only when it's your possessions that it becomes all too real, traumatic, and personal. That's when the deep emotions come out.

The key to sharing stories and memories is to have a good audience. Etta had one in me: I was genuinely interested in her, we had a good rapport, and we had lots of time. That allowed us to savor the events and people in her life. Whatever emotions you have while poring through your belongings are your emotions—they are valid and real. Embrace them. Your audience should share that same philosophy. In addition to your stories, sharing your *feelings* with another human being can be a deeply rewarding experience and is the key to letting go.

Now is the time to ask for or accept help. Many family, friends, and neighbors may offer to help; this is the time to take them up on it. They may not know how they can be helpful, so you can ask specifically: Can you come sit with me for a few hours as I go through one closet? Then tell your stories. A story is no good if you are telling it to yourself. Get an audience even if they aren't family. I promise they will find the stories of your life interesting.

Don't censor your stories. Tell them how you remember them, good or bad. The more details and honesty, the better. No one wants to hear about the old lady sitting in the corner clutching her purse making good choices—we want to remember the wild grandma who kissed a boy at Tantilla Gardens.

Etta eventually got rid of more than half of her stuff. As you'll see later in the book, that's roughly the ideal decluttering outcome. Etta decided to keep her most storied items—her Legacy List—including choice photos and home videos, a few pieces of old clothing and valuable jewelry, several toys that used to belong to a dog she had, and a table and chair she couldn't bear to part with. "It doesn't make me happy to keep things," she said, words whose wisdom I've only begun to understand as I age and appreciate a life with less.

For Etta, getting her stuff organized and packed up might have been useful and pleasant, maybe even emotionally gratifying. For me, however, working with Etta was a life-changing experience. Instead of just being a good Boy Scout and helping out an older woman, I had a transformative encounter. After we were done, she hugged me for a long time and then handed me a check for my services. I remember staring at it, thinking that *this* might be my future. A hug and a check. People would pay me to listen to their stories and help them through a transitional period of their lives? Could that be for real? It seemed like the answer to my prayers. This was special, this was real. That hug was a connection I hadn't felt in a long time. We shared a true moment in life together, and then I got enough money to pay my rent.

Days later, looking back on my time with Etta, I understood that this was what I wanted to do with my life, just this: Help people simplify their lives by realizing the value of their memories. Each human being comes programmed with his or her own memory card. The countless items stored on yours—

scenes from your childhood, feelings about your first job, the pain of your first love—are completely unique to you. They are what *make* you the individual that you are.

And that is how I became a professional declutterer. Within weeks after my work with Etta, I started a company, Clutter Cleaner, to help people like her. I had thought that most of my work would be to help people clear out their junk and maybe move. I soon learned that some clients needed help just figuring out where they were going. People like Lauren, whom you'll meet next.

STEP TWO
· · · · · · · · · · · ·
Define Your Finish Line

LAUREN WAS ONE OF MY first clients at Clutter Cleaner. She lived in Washington, D.C., about an hour and half's drive from Richmond without traffic—which means it's really a four-hour drive, because there's always traffic. Her real estate agent had told her about a youngish guy named Matt Paxton back in Richmond who could help her out. I drove up to meet her, excited that my reputation had so quickly spread out of state.

A retired schoolteacher, Lauren was a little under five feet tall, stout, in her midseventies. She was a widower, now living alone. Her husband, Stephen, I soon learned, had worked in intelligence—the CIA or FBI, I assumed, though she never said—and had passed away six years earlier. Her kids were grown and lived halfway across the country. She told me that she needed some help moving.

Her old brick home was lovely, with curved arched doorways and ten-foot-high ceilings. She was clearly devoted to her crafts: As I walked in, she pointed out colorful blankets she had cross-stitched, strewn in piles around the house. I was particularly impressed by a huge and elaborate dining set.

"So, where are you moving to?" I asked her, sitting on her screened-in back porch.

"I don't know yet," she responded, "but I'm ready to start decluttering."

I was confused—both she and her real estate agent had mentioned moving. But in fact, Lauren hadn't decided upon anything beyond talking to some moving experts, and even that was only at the behest of her kids. Lauren understood vaguely that she needed to move out of a big home she no longer needed. One of the first things she told me was that no matter what, two things were going with her wherever she went: her twenty-two-piece-set dining room table and dishes—above all, she loved to entertain, she said—and her cross-stitched blankets.

But she had never given much thought to what she might want her life to look like after moving out. She was focused on the needs of her daily life, not her vision for the future. She didn't assume she'd live in her current house forever. Rather, after Stephen died from a sudden heart attack, she'd figured she had a few more years before she needed to think about her next life stage. When a few years came and went, she added a few more years to her timeline. Only the intervention of her children convinced her to meet with Clutter Cleaner.

I've since heard the same story from thousands of clients. Deciding if and where to move can be enormously difficult—even paralyzing. (Witness my initial decision to stay put instead of picking up my family to move to Georgia!) That's why sometimes it's helpful to have someone like me on hand to help out. Working with Lauren helped me realize that part of my job is helping people envision their future and navigate the steps to get there. I completely understood her strategy of delaying those life-changing decisions. Decluttering before making the harder choices that can bring upheaval and uncertainty is an easy shortcut. But ultimately it's misguided.

WHAT ARE YOUR OPTIONS?

The first and most important question in downsizing is: Where are you going? What is your destination? Or, as we say in my business: What's the finish line? You may end up staying where you are and "aging in place," in industry parlance, or you may downsize to a smaller home. Probably half my clients stay put. The rest move, and some know before they call me where they're going. The point is, knowing where you are (or aren't) going gives you a better road map to decluttering. You'll be able to accomplish a lot more if you know where you're going. The smartest choices are those we make with careful planning and forethought. And if my clients aren't there yet, I help them get there.

Based on my personal and professional experiences, I've found that what keeps us from looking ahead is memories. Surprisingly, it's often not the fear of losing old memories that keeps us in place. Rather, we're afraid to let go and move on because we fear not making new memories in a different environment. We know the past and the present. We know what memories will be made here with the people we know in our current location. We know what memories we have already made here. But we don't know what memories we'll make and who—if anyone—we will make them with in our future locations. That's scary. You can't see forward when you are making this decision; you only see backward.

Sitting on Lauren's back porch, looking at her lovely flower garden, we talked about her fears of moving out of her home. That's what they were—fears. Of giving up her life. Of giving up her past. Of giving up her independence. As she opened up to me, we explored the many choices available to her. Lauren had not considered any options beyond nursing homes. Like a lot of people, in fact, she didn't know about many other options. Here are the choices I explored with her, as I've explored with so many other clients who call me before making a decision about where they're going next.

Staying Put

If your current home suits you, you can stay there. As you age, you can make modifications to the home, such as adding grab bars to showers and moving your bedroom to the main level. Staying in your home probably feels like the most comfortable and secure option. You're in your familiar neighborhood with your familiar belongings around you. You probably have a daily routine that feels comfortable. So long as you are healthy, you maintain your independence. If you need support in the future—from home and lawn maintenance to health care—you can hire help, if you can afford it. And if you own your home and your mortgage is paid, this can be the most affordable option.

This option is not for everyone. If you're living alone, aging in place can be lonely. If you need services in the future, such as home health care aides, you'll need to factor that into your budget. And structural changes to the home, such as adding ramps, widening doorways to accommodate wheelchairs, or putting handrails in the bathroom, can sometimes decrease the value of the home or the buying pool. Usually, prospective buyers aren't looking for homes renovated for aging in place. (Alternatively, these changes can be positive if you live in a region where more buyers want such renovations.)

Downsizing to a smaller place

Moving from a house to an apartment or condo is a common choice for individuals and couples who don't need as much space as they once did. You can also choose a place where someone else will shovel the snow, mow the lawn, and unclog the kitchen sink. Whether you move in the same neighborhood or across the country, this can be a new adventure.

Home-sharing

Lauren didn't want to live with her kids, but we explored other potential roommates. Home-sharing is one of my favorite housing options, because you have the company of roommates and you share costs while still enjoying independence. This is the obvious choice for multigenerational living, but it's also great for bunking up with pals or finding others in the same position looking for a new home. When people are well matched, home-sharing can be like creating a new family. If you're older, think of this as *The Golden Girls* in real life. Independent companies will match your personality traits with multiple compatible roommates for you to choose from and handle the legal and financial paperwork and payments. One of the companies I've worked with is Silvernest, which you can learn more about at www.silvernest.com.

Home-sharing isn't for those who prioritize their privacy above all else. If you choose this option and haven't lived with someone for a long time, it may take a while to adjust to having people in your living space. In addition, if you need services in the future, you'll have to move or bring in help.

Active adult independent living communities

One thing about Lauren was that she loved people. She lit up when I told her about independent living communities, housing designed exclusively for older adults, usually fifty-five-plus. The types of housing range widely, from apartments to detached condos and single-family homes. Some stand alone; others are part of communities with other levels of care (as I go into below). Independent living offers a great sense of community but also safety, independence, companionship, and activities. If there comes a time you need more services, you can hire them or move to a community that provides them.

Village networks

Villages are membership-driven, grassroots, nonprofit organizations run by volunteers and staff to help people stay in their homes by increasing access to services. You stay put and the Village coordinates services you may need—transportation, home repair, activities, and more. You get a sense of community and camaraderie while living independently. Generally, health care is not provided. You can find Villages throughout the country at www.vtvnetwork.org.

Assisted living

Lauren was fortunate to be in good health, but she also wanted to understand options should she begin to need help. We discussed assisted living communities, which are often small apartments in a single community composed of people who do not require round-the-clock medical care but want some day-to-day help with daily tasks such as getting dressed or performing housework. The meals, services, and activities available at assisted living facilities span widely between different communities.

Nursing homes/skilled nursing communities

This option is for people who need significant medical and custodial care (that is, care with general activities of daily living) but don't need to be in a hospital. You'll be in good company, as nearly 1.5 million people receive care in a nursing home. Unfortunately, nursing homes can be expensive, averaging $90,000 per year. Still, they are often less expensive than paying for twenty-four-hour care in your home.

Continuing care retirement communities (CCRCs)

Continuing care retirement communities offer long-term care options for people who want to stay in the same place through different phases of the aging process. CCRCs generally have levels for independent living, assisted living, skilled nursing, and sometimes memory care. About two-thirds charge an entry fee, sometimes refundable, which can be hefty—on average $329,000, but fees can top $1 million at some communities. Others operate on a rental basis with lower to no up-front fees. Care, meals, and activities are available on-premises, providing a sense of stability and familiarity as a resident's abilities or health conditions change. Many offer private spaces to rent so residents can entertain. In the CCRCs my clients have moved to, the food options are plentiful and delicious.

NARROWING YOUR OPTIONS

Several glasses of wine and mugs of coffee later, Lauren opened up to me about her finances, which are critical to making wise decisions. It turned out Lauren was lucky: She confided that she had the resources to move anywhere she wanted. For many people, their finances limit their choices. In some cases, moving in with family members is the only affordable option. Factor into your decision the money you have for decluttering consultants, packers, and movers.

As we talked, Lauren's vision slowly came into focus. She admitted that keeping up with the cleaning and yard work was too much. She also admitted to feeling a little lonely in the big, empty house. Her home was terrific for a family, but now she basically used just four rooms: the bedroom, bathroom, kitchen, and living room. We talked a lot about loneliness. That, I've learned over the years, has helped guide people's decisions in where they move.

And we continued to talk about her fears. Like so many people, Lauren lived under the misconception that moving into housing designed for older people meant that she would have to live in some cold, depressing asylum. She envisioned the type she saw on old TV shows like *Murder She Wrote* or *Matlock*: places with full-time supervised care, meals, and activities.

We spoke about how she wouldn't be giving up control of her life. She was *taking* control. That's what planning and decision making provide us with—control over our own lives. When we procrastinate, or simply avoid making a decision at all, we are giving up the ability to control our own destiny. In fact, because of the fear of losing control, we are actually losing control by *not* taking action on our own.

I told Lauren I would love to work with her, but until she settled on an outcome, Clutter Cleaner could only sort some of her things. Beyond that, we couldn't be of much help. As we talked, it became clear that Lauren didn't want to leave her home, even as she acknowledged that she was feeling isolated and wanted a stronger social network. She looked at items she'd had for sixty years—where to even *start* thinking about letting go of some of that stuff? I've learned that it's much easier for someone to sort through books than it is to make a decision about the next phase of life. Over the decades, Lauren and her family had built a wonderful life in the place she had called home for many years. She had raised her children between those walls, enjoyed a wonderful marriage there. She was terrified at the thought of losing control over her life. Better to keep things as they were, she thought, vacillating, delaying, ignoring, even if the situation was becoming untenable. Her strong sense of pride and fear of losing control over her day-to-day life kept her in a place she knew was no longer right for her.

Eventually, though, Lauren told me she wanted to look into alternative living options where she could enjoy companionship. I told her we could find a place that would offer her an even better social life than she was currently enjoying! That's the beauty of housing options—there are so many of them, catered to fit whatever you're looking for.

After consulting some friends about where they live, Lauren decided that she wanted to move into an active fifty-five-plus independent living community. This wasn't an easy decision for her, and it isn't easy for anyone—it's a major life choice, one that involves leaving the past behind. Her announcement counted as major progress, and I was very proud of her.

"That's the plan," she said.

But really, that was the extent of her plan. She didn't yet know exactly *where* she was moving to. You can't even pack well for a vacation, let alone a move, if you don't know the details of where you'll be going. That would have to be our next decision.

PLACEMENT AGENCIES

I didn't know about them at the time, but now that I have more experience, I would have recommended that Lauren meet with a senior placement agency. These are companies that work with older people and their families to consider the various housing options. Here's what you need to know about placement agencies.

Placement agencies are usually a free service to consumers; communities pay the fees upon placement. Agencies help individuals and families find the best place for them, taking into account finances, location, social preferences, medical needs, and other factors. Placement agencies can be a lifeline, providing expert guidance on housing options. But be sure to select a company that works with as many communities as possible—and note that they probably don't work with smaller communities. If they only work with a few and are paid directly by them, they might not have your best interests in mind. You don't want a company that prioritizes its bottom line over your well-being. Research the agencies and look at their online customer ratings. Just as you would with an accountant or lawyer, interview multiple placement agencies to find the right fit for you and your family.

VISIT FIRST

Here's one piece of advice I tell my clients: Before moving, visit the places you're considering—whether in town, in another state, or in another country. Visit for at least a few days, if you can. Let me take a brief detour to explain why.

Despite spending most of high school running track, I managed to graduate in 1993. I informed my dad that I wanted to attend the University of Richmond because that was where the Richmond Spiders basketball team played. He told me to visit the campus and check out two things: the student parking lot and the faculty parking lot. Although I didn't understand his reasoning, I followed his advice. When I walked through the student lot, I saw that it was packed with Mercedes-Benzes, BMWs, and SUVs. Fancy cars, all. The faculty lot, meanwhile, had cars most people drive. In fact, I even saw a maroon 1984 Honda Accord, which I proudly drove. It was clear that instead of the heaven that I imagined it to be, the University of Richmond would not be a good fit for me. Instead, I opted for something humbler, a small place called Mary Washington College (now called the University of Mary Washington). It proved to be an excellent decision, and it came about only because I visited both schools. And figuring out the right college is a decision about where to spend just four years—a move to a new place involves a choice about where to spend decades, ideally.

To narrow down her choices, Lauren talked to some friends who lived in senior communities about what they liked and didn't like. Indeed, word of mouth is a great way to learn about what can work for you. She took the time to visit several places, which helped narrow down her choices and refine her needs. I always advise my clients to speak with residents of the different places they visit to understand their likes and dislikes—who knows better about a community than the people who live there? Some research can be conducted online, but there is no substitute for in-person research. The good news is, a group of eightyish-year-old individuals have no problem telling you the brutally honest truth. You'll know pretty quickly if you want to move there or not. Invite a friend or relative to explore with you. Other ways to gather important information include driving or taking public transit around communities where you're considering living.

Finally, after more research, Lauren narrowed down her decision even further. She settled on a nearby continuing care retirement community in Ashburn, Virginia, that had robust active independent living. It sat on a gorgeous, sprawling campus, with twelve restaurants, a health club, and many other amenities. We were getting close.

Her next decision: One bedroom or two? This, I've found, is another critical choice. How much do you want to downsize at

MATT'S TOP TEN TIPS FOR CHOOSING A NEW HOME

1. Choose your new space by deciding on the life you want to live there.
2. If you're older and thinking ahead, get started early on transitioning; the longer you wait, the fewer options you may have. It's never too soon to start looking.
3. Calculate the budget you have available to spend. Understanding your finances will help determine the places where you can move and your ability to afford things like decluttering consultants, movers, and packers.
4. Speak with friends, relatives, neighbors, and people in your worship community and clubs about where they live and what they like and don't like about it.
5. Consider what you want in a home. To that end, tap into the quick and easy tools in *Wise Moves: Checklist for*

this point? She couldn't figure out what was better for her. She didn't want to spend more money than was necessary, but she was concerned that the one-bedroom might be too small for her and her belongings, especially her crafting materials and twenty-two-piece dining room set. A two-bedroom, on the other hand, might be harder to maintain, and the extra space might make her feel lonely.

Where to Live, What to Consider, and Whether to Stay or Go, available wherever books are sold.

6. Drive around the neighborhoods and towns you're considering.
7. Once you've identified a few options, visit them, preferably with family or friends, ideally multiple times. If you're thinking of moving to another area altogether, whether another part of the country, a different country, or a new community, try to stay a few days or weeks before you make your decision.
8. Get a floor plan of the new space you'll be moving into. If one isn't available, have a measuring tape handy to work out precise measurements, down to the inch.
9. Figure out how much of your current furniture and other stuff will fit into your new surroundings.
10. Consider not positioning all your old objects to recreate the same space; that's a way of moving backward, not forward.

Being new to my work still, I didn't immediately clue in that Lauren's uncertainty about her destination would become a problem. I thought it would be enough for us to know that there was *somewhere* she was going. She was adamant that the dining set and dishes join her in her new home, along with the mountains of beautiful blankets she had made. For Lauren, I understood, entertaining others and crafting were intrinsic to who she was. Asking her to abandon all that would be like asking her to abandon her values. We packed it all up.

MEASURE BY MEASURE

Lauren finally settled on an eight-hundred-square-foot one-bedroom apartment in the CCRC. She was determined to squeeze everything from her four-thousand-square-foot home into her new apartment. Because I was just starting out, Lauren and I failed to do something that I now find essential: Get a floor plan of the new living space and measure spaces meticulously. Even if two spaces have the same square footage, they can be configured differently. In time, I have realized that moving is in some ways a math problem—understanding the geometry of a place is a prerequisite to furnishing and decorating it properly. The same thing is true of downsizing and decluttering; the space in any given area is finite and usually fixed, so the physical items must be limited, too. It's important to understand exactly what you must have and where it will fit before you know exactly what to get rid of. If possible, have a measuring tape handy to work out precise measurements, down to the inch. You'll want to use every bit of space you have in the most efficient way possible.

Few of us want to end up like a woman I once worked with on *Hoarders* who had packed her stuff from floor to ceiling so tightly that it was impossible to move around.

BE SMART ABOUT STORAGE

I often see people decide to move and get some things out of their house only if they can keep in storage everything they're not taking to their new home. Before you make the same mistake, here's a cautionary word about storage.

With nearly fifty thousand units across the United States, storage is a $40 billion industry. You might have seen *Storage Wars*, a reality show on A&E about people who bid on leftover storage contents. That show focuses on the people buying the leftover stuff, but the reality is that millions of people wind up paying for the storage for years—only to abandon the items in the end.

I once had a client who paid $385 a month to store her antique furniture, which was worth about $25,000 when it went in. That was twenty-five years earlier. In all, she spent $115,500 on the unit: $385 a month for twenty-five years. When we retrieved the furniture, it had decayed somewhat, but we could still sell it—for only $5,000. So, yes, I encourage people to try to fit what you must store in your existing home.

The smartest way to use storage is not to use it at all. Your home is already one giant storage unit, and you pay a lot for it, either in taxes and mortgage payments or rent. Anything you need should fit in there. I use the principle of "equal in, equal out": If your home is full, discard an item (equal size or shape) for any new one.

I can hear you trying to argue with me; I get it. Obviously certain situations merit short-term storage, such as when you're renovating, or you're moving into a new place that isn't ready yet. But it should only be used as a last resort. And even then, use it wisely. If you must use storage:

- **Rent the smallest unit available.** This will force you to economize and get rid of unnecessary items. And if it isn't important enough to be in your home, it's likely not that important. I list some storage places in the Resources section at the back of this book.
- **Impose a time limit.** The shorter, the better. Nobody imagines that they will keep something in a locker for twenty years, but it happens—month by month, year by year. But if you set a deadline of, say, six months or one

year, when the time comes it'll be easier for you to admit that you can do without that bicycle you swore you'd get around to riding again one day.

- **Choose a unit a few flights up.** The most expensive storage units are those that let you drive right up to them. You'll get much more bang for your buck with an upstairs unit— and needing to schlep stuff up and down stairs may convince you to store less of it.

- **Pay by the item.** There are new types of storage companies that let you pay by the item, a process called "on-demand storage." Your skis won't require a ten-by-ten unit if the storage company will give you a price for just the item alone— and deliver it to you when you want it. Many of these are run on apps for your phone—you just let the company know which item you want delivered and when you want it, and the item shows up the next day. If you don't need the full storage unit, these are worth the money and space saved.

- **Don't feel guilty if you can't live without storage! It just means you're not ready to handle the emotions that come with separating from items important to you.** But one day you will be. Storage is, at best, a stepping-stone. It's a way of delaying the reckoning that comes with decluttering.

RECREATE FAMILIARITY, OR MIX THINGS UP?

Lauren also confronted a dilemma that's typical for anyone who is moving: whether you want to recreate your old setup or devise a new one. Should the bed go in the same place in the new bedroom as it was in the old? What about the night table or dresser? Should she buy new furniture entirely? Recreating the old setup offers the benefits of familiarity at a time of profound instability and change. Nevertheless, I advise clients to take advantage of a move or downsize to establish a new setup; moving is an adventure, a time for closing chapters and new beginnings. If you can afford to, splurge for some new stuff. I find that having a few new pillows makes anybody appreciate the new surroundings more. Even more extravagant? Spring for a new bedspread and mattress!

Clutter Cleaner worked closely with Lauren on her move, and I wish I could say that the story ended there and move on to the next chapter of this book.

But, as you might suspect, Lauren's stuff didn't quite fit into her new place. Her dining set took up the whole living room, leaving no space to move around it. Dozens of her homemade cross-stitched blankets decorated every surface. (Fortunately, I was able to talk her out of putting the trophy case filled with them into the bathroom—because, she mysteriously reasoned, "that's where all my visitors will be sitting anyway.")

As Lauren got settled, a shift occurred. Meeting and party rooms available in her new community convinced her to sell off the dishes and dining room table and chairs that just weeks earlier she had sworn she couldn't live without. Instead, she decided she wanted a room dedicated to crafting—her passion. These were huge decisions, and they were different than choices she'd made earlier. That's the power of decluttering, downsizing, and moving—we discover new parts of ourselves even as we shed our old skins. Lauren ditched the dining set and upgraded to a two-bedroom apartment, where there would be space for a hobby room.

Lauren didn't decide how she wanted to live until the *end* of the first move. Ideally, we would have designed her entire move around those decisions. But better late than never. Lesson learned.

In reality, most people go in the wrong order: They try to sell their home first, then they are rushed to declutter. They're forced to move quickly because the house either has to be shown or gets sold. That makes the entire process rushed, leaving them little time to think about the life they actually want to have in the new space. But really, that's what matters: the new life you want. Not the stuff you take with you.

I am glad to say that Lauren's story has a happy ending: She got to keep her trophy case. She moved it to her crafting room so she could proudly display her work for herself and visitors to enjoy. She loves the new friends in her building and told me she lives a more active social life than ever before. I felt good on the day we unpacked her belongings in the two-bedroom apartment; she left us to finish unpacking while she scurried off to join some new friends for dinner.

The reality is that Lauren's evolution from being fearful of moving to excited about her new place is entirely typical. It's how it feels when we're staring down the barrel of getting rid of that favorite side table, our Lladró collection, or those first-edition leather-bound books our grandparents gave us—even though they're now cracked and disintegrating and, honestly, we've never read them. The physical process of decluttering and downsizing is a lot of work, but the harder battle is fighting through the emotional and psychological barriers. As Lauren proved, though, we can overcome those barriers with courage, resilience, and information. She's lucky it happened so fast; other clients have taken longer to settle in.

But Lauren also had an advantage: Once she settled on

THE KEY TO MOVING ON

Lauren and I were able to make a breakthrough because we spoke sensitively but honestly about her deepest fears regarding her future, her past, her community, and her autonomy. She was clear about her desires to connect socially and continue crafting, and she was candid about her budget. By walking her through the many options available to her, I succeeded in helping her understand that she was in control of the process every step of the way. When she ultimately made her choice, it was the right one for her—because she was the one who'd made it, after considering all the options and doing due diligence. That was only possible because Lauren told me the story that was her life. My job is to help people write the next chapter in those stories.

moving, she knew she wanted to get rid of everything besides her crafts, dining set, and dishes. As you'll see in the next chapter, not everyone is so fortunate in knowing what they want to keep and what they want to get rid of. Figuring that out can be an agonizing process. Let's walk through it together.

Take the First Baby Steps

MAGGIE WAS ON OVERLOAD WHEN she phoned me in August 2007.

"I'm ready to run away and join a convent," she confided, which wasn't realistic because she was happily married and four months' pregnant. But she and her husband, Jesse, both in their midtwenties, had been living in a small apartment in Richmond when Jesse's parents died suddenly in a car crash. Now Jesse was traumatized by losing his parents, and on top of that, he and Maggie were overwhelmed by the logistics of inheriting his family home, passed down from his grandparents to his parents and now to him, packed with generations of stuff.

About six months before she called me, Maggie, a schoolteacher, and Jesse, a U.S. Army veteran who had just finished law school, had moved from their small apartment in the city into his parents' two-thousand-square-foot house in an up-and-coming suburb. It was the perfect starter home for them: two bedrooms, good schools nearby, a perfect green lawn, and the all-important white picket fence. It was a dream home.

Well, it *should* have been a dream home. But three generations' worth of stuff was all crammed under one roof. I was into my fifth year of decluttering by then, but even I wasn't prepared for the state of the house.

I literally couldn't see the dining room table because it was covered with dishes; CDs; vintage vinyl records; clothing; boxes; magazines; mail (a mix of important documents, junk mail, and sympathy and Christmas cards); and God knows what else. The rest of the home was similarly chaotic, bursting at the seams with furniture, dishes, clothes, even car parts. There was barely enough room to move around.

This would have been a formidable challenge for anyone. But just after they moved in, Maggie and Jesse learned that Maggie was pregnant. On top of the grief, they had to make space for their new life with their soon-to-be bundle of joy. The precious time in their lives was still very much a painful one. By the time they brought me in, Maggie felt desperate and Jesse felt depressed. They couldn't get started.

Jesse and Maggie weren't alone in feeling stuck. Many people I work with don't know how or where to begin decluttering, because they feel overpowered and overmatched by the immense jumble that is their living space. This chapter is going to help you understand how to leave the starting gate, and outline some of the initial steps I recommend taking when you're feeling just plain overwhelmed.

THE TEN-MINUTE SWEEP

We needed to dig in. I went with my secret weapon, the "Ten-Minute Sweep." You clean for ten minutes every night, five nights a week. Take the weekends off, if you need to—and if you're going through tough emotions at the same time, you definitely need that time off. Emotionally, you can't expect to part in hours or days with objects you've had for years or even decades. That's especially true when you're going through up-heaval in your life. Jesse was facing huge changes in a short time: a new career, newly married, new baby, and the loss of both parents. All those events are difficult on their own. Facing them in a short span at a young age? Forget it.

You can't clean in one weekend a house that's been lived in for thirty years. That's not realistic—but you can clean for ten minutes. *That's* realistic. And it's realistic for your situation, too.

Because one of the reasons you likely bought this book is you've been carrying this emotional and physical baggage around for so long.

I suggested that Maggie and Jesse do their work in bite-size ten-minute blocks, the same time every day. I remember seeing a look of relief come over Jesse's face when I suggested that. "Ten minutes!" he said. "*That* I can handle." (Though honestly, when I'm working directly with clients, we usually go far over that limit once we get working.) This is yet another reason why giving yourself time is essential to effective downsizing and decluttering: It puts less stress on you by offering you more breathing room. Once I outlined the Ten-Minute Sweep, I could see the tension leave Jesse's face, along with much of the guilt he'd felt over his difficulties decluttering for the past months.

I took this moment to talk to them about what I call "Pompeii hoards." Like the ritzy ancient Roman city of Pompeii, which was covered by volcanic ash, Pompeii hoards are normal, clean homes that have been smothered by multiple generations' worth of stuff. First, there was his parents' stuff, accumulated in the home they'd lived in for three decades. His parents, it turned out, had also kept many possessions they inherited from *their* parents. There was enough furniture for three homes jammed together in one small house. On top of that were the belongings Jesse and Maggie had brought with them from their apartment. The city of Pompeii was destroyed by the ash, and I've seen homes destroyed by Pompeii hoards, too. The Ten-Minute Sweep to the rescue!

The Ten-Minute Sweep comes with a single catch, however: It only works if you stick to it. If you're not careful, ten minutes per day can easily become five minutes per day, which soon becomes zero minutes per day, or fifty minutes one day a week. You can't let happen. Nope. I've seen this happen time and again. The Ten-Minute Sweep works not only because it's an easy lift, but because you get in the habit of decluttering. You need to commit to those ten minutes until it becomes part of your daily routine.

Once we did our first Ten-Minute Sweep, we headed to a nearby pub for a few beers, a part of the process I highly recommend! Jesse explained to me that while we were doing our work together, he was faced with reminders of what he'd just lost: photographs of his grandparents when they emigrated from Italy to the United States. His father's records and saxophone. His mother's board games and prize-winning paintings. There were treasured artifacts from Jesse's childhood: macaroni art from kindergarten, birthday cards, favorite toys, and athletic trophies. There was gear from his tours in Iraq. It was a delicate time to sift through all that, plucking items to keep and discarding others.

Jesse and I talked about our loss and pain, about how grief could be so enveloping that going through it made carrying out basic tasks difficult, let alone sifting through the intimate possessions of a loved one who'd just died. Like me, Jesse didn't really have any choice about decluttering—I wish everyone could cull through their family's objects while all our family members are still with us. But not everyone has that luxury. Sometimes you just need to make it happen.

SET A DEADLINE

You need to commit to deadlines, too. Deadlines help hold us accountable and force us to do the hard work even when we might not feel like it. If I did the dishes only when I felt like it, my home would be full of dirty dishes. But because I know the dishes *must* be cleaned, I somehow muster the energy to do them. The deadline can be days, weeks, or months, but I recommend not giving yourself a limit of more than four to five months. Any longer than that and it's easy to delay the project entirely. Depending on the size and scope of a project, a two- to three-month deadline is usually more than enough. In Maggie and Jesse's case, the deadline was five months: the baby's due date. We *had* to get this done. This young couple needed not only to clear tons of space, but they also had to make it safe for an infant, a tiny, curious being who would soon find electric sockets or hidden compartments to stick his or her fingers into. That required getting started, no matter how unfortunate the timing. As if to remind everyone of that, the baby would give Maggie a good kick now and then.

But, I hear you say, *Ten minutes won't be enough! I'll need years!* First, the ten-minute rule is just to get you in the habit of decluttering. Once you get into the swing of things, you'll find yourself taking on larger chunks of time voluntarily. Second, you'll be amazed at how much you can get done in ten minutes of hard, thoughtful work. Just give it a shot.

UNDERSTAND YOUR WHY

One of the first things I like to say to new clients is: *Understand your why.* What are the reasons you want to get the clutter out of your life? Are you looking to have less stress in your life? Or do you just need more space for your stuff? If you're moving, are you hoping to pare down your belongings, or do you want to take everything with you? Or are you making room for a friend to come live in the house? Be as specific as possible in your objectives because your goals are what you'll return to again and again for focus and motivation whenever you get stuck. You can't win a race when you don't know where the finish line is. And you'll probably wind up running a lot more than you need to. Maybe pull a muscle, too.

Maggie and Jesse were clear on their main goal: Make enough space for their growing family. "There's just too much stuff here," Maggie said to me. Jesse reluctantly agreed, though that admission meant he'd eventually have to make some tough choices. But what did too much stuff mean exactly? I encouraged them to nail down the specifics.

I asked them question after question, and we all listened to their responses so together we could solve the problem. Did they want *only* their own stuff in the house? Or were they thinking of hanging on to some of what they inherited? Would just cleaning out the den for a playroom be enough, or did they want more space in the bedrooms and kitchen? What about clearing space to renovate the kitchen? I asked them if they were planning on having more children—if so, the time to declutter for a second child would be now, not in a year or two, when there would be a toddler running around creating havoc, depriving them of time and energy. Sure, life is unpredictable and full of surprises. But while it's impossible to anticipate all the hiccups and challenges that come our way, we tried to envision what they wanted in the future and how to create a home that could accommodate their dreams.

CHOOSE A SPACE THAT SETS YOU UP FOR SUCCESS

Don't feel that you need to tackle the hardest parts in your home first. In fact, I recommend doing just the opposite. Confronting that cluttered attic or garage can feel overwhelming and discouraging because seeing progress can be difficult. Nothing is worse than looking at a giant mountain you're going to climb and feeling like you'll never get to the peak. You feel so deflated at the impossibility of getting there that you give up and instead go for pancakes at the nearby diner. So remember this: You are taking one step at a time. The rest of the mountain will be there, and you don't need to stare at it or worry about how you'll climb it. Start with clearing out a junk drawer, a box from the garage, a small pantry, the guest room closet, or even just one particular corner of the attic. But here's another of my secret weapons: Whatever your situation is, start with a task you'll be able to finish and feel good—even elated—about your very first day. When space appears where clutter once was, it seems almost magical. It's deeply encouraging at a point when encouragement is greatly needed.

I mentioned that every inch of Jesse and Maggie's home was jammed with mountains of stuff, but that's not exactly accurate. To Jesse, it wasn't stuff; it was a living memorial to the family he'd just lost. He didn't know where or how to begin climbing the mountain.

Maggie suggested we start with the den. She wanted to move quickly—there wasn't even enough space to hold a baby shower! But Jesse's blood drained from his face when he heard Maggie's proposition. I could easily sympathize with both of their perspectives; they each had valid points, anxieties, and needs. We had to balance both of their inclinations. And I always tried to remember that, no matter what, their baby was still on its way. I've had babies and I've learned from personal experience that they don't wait for us to be ready for them.

I told them that we wanted to choose a space that sets you up for success. By starting small and limiting our initial time commitment, we would be setting daily goals that we could actually reach. I suggested the dining room table. Just being able to see and use it would count as meaningful progress for us, and with all three of us working together, we could be there in a few days. We needed to start somewhere, after all.

Another reason I opted to start with the table was that it would be relatively easy emotionally. Jesse told me that they'd mostly had their family dinners in the kitchen when he was growing up, with the dining room reserved for company. That made it less connected to precious memories than other spaces in the house were. Things like clothes, diaries, photographs, smoking pipes, or a musical instrument can be excruciating to go through, especially when we're grieving. Those items are so unique, so personal. But looking at Jesse's parents' table, it was clear that it was mostly just a table, even to him. We went to work on it.

DON'T DELAY, START RIGHT AWAY

I suggested that we start specifically with the paper on the dining room table. There were several trees' worth of useless paper there. The junk mail quickly went into the recycling bin. Then there were newsletters and newspapers and magazines. I told Jesse that if by now you haven't read them, you're never going to. And that's okay. It's always best to accept reality. Within just a few minutes, we began to make a significant dent in the blanket of paper covering the table. It had looked more imposing than it really was.

The truth is, when we see clutter, the volume we see usually has a lot of air in it. Sometimes it's just poorly stacked and takes up a lot of space. A simple reorganizing can often make a huge difference. Just clearing up the space on the table provided valuable encouragement to Jesse and Maggie. It showed them that we could actually make a decluttered home happen. What had seemed impossible to them was in fact possible. Jesse perked up, and Maggie gave me a nice compliment: "Now I know why you're called the Clutter Cleaner." When I'd come up with the name, I still thought the work I was doing was about helping people clean. Packing and unpacking. Some organizing. Maybe sweeping up, too. Now I know better. My job is more about helping people achieve peace of mind than anything else. It's a psychological and even spiritual process that I help facilitate.

NO, YOU REALLY DON'T NEED MORE STUFF

Jesse got a bit nervous as we all lugged the magazines to the front porch in boxes. "Maybe we should get a label maker for all this stuff," he said. "Or put them in some bins instead of cardboard boxes?"

I understood the impulse. It was clear what he was getting

at, although I don't think he knew it—he wanted to buy organizing supplies as a way to avoid the scary feeling of starting to declutter. But I told him that he didn't need to buy a bunch of bins and fancy labeling systems. More important, he shouldn't! *Getting more stuff is a particularly bad way to have less stuff.* Indeed, for many people, too much consumption is what got us into our cluttered situation in the first place.

Don't make the same mistake of oversupplying yourself with materials for decluttering or downsizing. Avoid buying tons of fancy baskets, plastic totes, plastic bags, label makers, and fancy organizing systems that stores will try to sell you. All these tools have their uses on occasion, but I believe that you can organize and declutter with the materials you already have in your home, and you'll probably use a lot less than you think. Make sure your intention to purchase supplies or planning materials isn't really a form of procrastination in disguise. I offer a complete list of what you'll need for cleaning, packing, and moving in Steps Eight and Nine.

THE ONE-MONTH RULE

As we moved yet another book from the dining room table to the donation pile, Jesse asked me a good question: "What if I need it later?" Often people tell me that they want to preserve their stuff because they think that one day down the line they might need it. It's true that to some degree, whenever we declutter, downsize, or move, we can't entirely predict what we'll need in the future. But the default shouldn't be to assume that we'll need everything we have.

Here's what I always recommend: If you know you'll use it within one month, keep it. Not six months, one year, or two years. One month. If you won't use it within one month, the odds are you won't use it at all. And the best predictor of whether you'll need an item is whether you are currently using it or have recently used it. Not whether you think that, one day, somehow, somewhere, you'll use it. Because that day, in all likelihood, will never come. The only exceptions to that rule are with seasonal clothes, recreational equipment, and holiday decorations. With seven kids between us, my wife and I have lots of expensive sporting equipment that gets used a lot during the summer, so we keep it stored out of the way of daily traffic. Also, an admission: I keep far too many holiday lights because we love Christmas. Because sometimes fun and family are more important than a perfectly clean home.

ASK PEOPLE YOU KNOW FOR HELP

I told Maggie and Jesse that they had done one really important thing right: They had phoned me! Seriously, it's not easy to know if and when to ask for help. So, know this: If you can get help, do so. People in your life may vaguely ask, "Can I help out?" Or they'll ask, "What can I do to help?" Well, this is the time in life to say "Yes—and here's how!" Maybe you can tap family, friends, or neighbors. Maybe it's people from your worship community or your softball team, or even your social media friends. Having someone present keeps you accountable and moving forward, just like it does with exercise (well, so I've heard). It also makes moving anything heavier much, much easier, making it less likely that someone will injure themselves.

Here's the biggest reason to have someone on hand to help out: to provide the audience I've already talked so much about. Jesse needed someone to talk to who *wasn't* his wife, since she had heard all his stories countless times. On that first afternoon and throughout the following days and weeks, Jesse and I bonded emotionally over his loss. Suffering the loss of a loved one is of course something I would never wish on anyone, but the one silver lining that grief offers is an ability to connect with another person's grief. The only reason I can offer this guidance to my clients is that it comes from experience.

ASK FOR PROFESSIONAL HELP

Of course, hiring a professional is different than asking a friend for help, since it'll cost you some money. But for anyone who can afford it, getting professional help may be well worth it, whether you're decluttering, downsizing, or moving. Here are the marquee players that I've worked with—and to be fully transparent, for much of my career, I've been a member of both organizations:

- **The National Association of Senior & Specialty Move Managers (NASMM.org).** Move managers certified by the National Association of Senior & Specialty Move Managers meet strict vetting requirements and time in the field. Don't let the name fool you: NASMM is for everyone, *not* just seniors. And it's not just for someone moving—these move managers work with people decluttering and downsizing, too. What *are* move managers? They're like coaches who help you every step of the way, from end to end. A moving company will just pack up anything you say and move your things. NASMM move managers do all the other stuff: advise you on the best ways to accomplish your objectives and help you sort, donate, sell, trash, and even recycle your items. They'll also help you hire movers, set up your new place, and pack and unpack. I've worked with hundreds of members of NASMM over the last twenty-plus years, and a few have become mentors and true friends.

- **The National Association of Productivity & Organizing Professionals (NAPO.net).** With more than thirty-five hundred members, the National Association of Productivity & Organizing Professionals is one of the world's biggest membership groups for decluttering and moving experts. While NASMM helps you move the stuff out of your house and into a new part of your life, NAPO focuses more on the stuff staying in your house, making it an ideal choice for those looking to get rid of some clutter. NAPO also is ideal for hoarding issues and has its own university to train its members, educating them in ethics, techniques, and best practices.

Many professionals are members of both NAPO and NASMM, as I was. Both of these organizations were started by women acting out of necessity—they found themselves in need of decluttering, downsizing, and moving assistance with their own families but couldn't find the appropriate, high-quality services. So those women started companies, and decades later it's an industry. That might be why they're so good. Crucially, they both charge by the hour, which means that you don't have to shell out thousands of dollars for a consultation, as you might for other companies. They're surprisingly affordable for the quality of the work they do. In addition, many members from each organization have decades of experience, so they have an unparalleled Rolodex of everyone in this business. They know the best junk haulers, the best moving companies, the top cleaning experts and repair people. Whenever I work with them, anywhere in the country, they seem to have the best contacts for local assistance.

Watch out for scammers in this line of work. In my years, I've seen some con artists, shysters, and people just plain bad at their jobs, working independently and making good money. You want to shop around for the best person or team. Since a move manager is like a personal coach, it's important to find one you connect with. This professional will get into your space and may be someone you're consulting over weeks and months. Go with your gut; if a move manager doesn't feel right for you, he probably isn't, even if he has good credentials. These people will hear some of your deepest and personal stories and will spend hours with you and your family. You want someone you like!

KEEP TALKING

After we'd finished with the dining room table, Jesse told me he was hesitant to clear out the stuff throughout the house belonging to his parents and grandparents. I asked him how he felt about potentially selling, donating, or throwing out some of the old furniture, ceramics, or art that he inherited.

"It feels like we'd be getting rid of *them*," he told me, referring to his family members. I've always remembered that line, because it speaks to the incredible power that objects have for us when they are intimately associated with people. That's why Lincoln's top hat is in the Smithsonian National Museum of American History—because Honest Abe is unimaginable without his signature garb. Having due respect for the emotional resonance of items—items that might look to outsiders like just random stuff or even junk—is essential to anyone decluttering, whether individuals or the professionals they bring in. As the saying goes, one person's trash is another person's treasure. I spoke Jesse's language, and that made all the difference.

MATT'S FOUR TIPS ON FINDING DECLUTTERING, DOWNSIZING, OR MOVING EXPERTS

Remember that you don't have to do all this work on your own. Experts out there can help you.

1. Research nearby professionals online through professional organizations such as NASMM and NAPO.
2. Ask friends, family, and neighbors for personal recommendations.
3. Don't assume experts are too expensive. Factor in the cost of your time if you would do it on your own.
4. Interview three or four experts before settling on the right one. Explain your needs and ask them questions such as:

- How many people have you worked with?
- Can you provide local references?
- Have you ever worked with clients in comparable situations to mine?
- What are your fees and how do you charge?
- What is your schedule and availability?

- Do you work alone or in teams?
- How would you deal with things I'd like to sell, donate, or recycle? Do you charge an additional fee for those services?
- What is your cancellation policy?
- What is the fee to postpone or reschedule?
- What part of the process does your insurance cover, what additional insurance will I need, and how can I purchase additional coverage?
- What are the services you provide? Services can include:
  - Planning a move
  - Organizing, sorting, and downsizing
  - Providing customized floor plans of the new home
  - Arranging to sell remaining items through auction, estate sale, consignment—or donating and providing an itemized receipt or tax valuation
  - Interviewing, scheduling, and overseeing movers
  - Arranging shipments and storage
  - Supervising professional packing
  - Unpacking items and setting up the new home
  - Arranging for a cleaning service, painters, and repair people to get the house ready for sale
  - Assisting in finding a real estate broker

FREE YOURSELF FROM GUILT

Once the dining room table seemed to magically reappear after its clutter was removed, Maggie was full steam ahead. She was heartened by our progress, small as it was. But Jesse remained heavyhearted. He looked around and saw a museum celebrating his parents and grandparents. He told me that he still felt guilty, that he still felt he was betraying his family by getting rid of some of their stuff.

I've found that guilt to be very common. We think we're expected to carry on not just traditions passed down to us from our families, friends, and communities, but their actual belongings. But the reality is that you aren't obligated to any thing or lifestyle other than the one you want. That's what this is about: building the life you want, not the life you think you should have or that you think a loved one would want you to have.

To make this happen, you need to be kind to yourself by allowing yourself to let go of expectations about your obligations to inanimate objects. Nobody else can give you that gift—it's something that *you* have to do for you. But whether it's items you inherited, as in Jesse's case, or items you've kept for twenty years, stop beating yourself up about moving on without them. Don't feel guilty for giving something away that your great-aunt gave you when you were eighteen. You are sixty-five, and she's been dead for thirty years—she is probably okay with it. But fair warning: Giving yourself a permission slip to let go of things also means letting yourself feel deep, powerful emotions. I tell all my clients, "This is real to you, so whatever emotion you have, it's valid and real. Embrace it." The physical process of decluttering and downsizing is a lot of work, but the harder battle is fighting through the emotional and psychological barriers. As Jesse stared at his father's baseball bat in his hands, I asked what he thought his parents would want for him. He looked at me and said softly that he knew they would want him to be happy, to make this into *his* home, to start a new life with his growing family there. That, not oversight of a museum for their belongings, was what they wanted for him.

LOVING WHO YOU ACTUALLY ARE

Sometimes guilt about our loved ones' belongings isn't what's inhibiting us from downsizing or decluttering. Instead, we're reluctant to give up on our visions about ourselves. This includes the fancy home-gym equipment that's never been used, that sporting equipment from a time long ago, and the clothes that you will never fit into again. (For years I deluded myself by holding on to one pair of size 30 jeans from my twenties. I will not confirm if they are stonewashed.) We have to force ourselves to say goodbye to our "fantasy self" items, the stuff that we think we'll use when we're different versions of ourselves. Sometimes we imagine ourselves to be different people, instead of admitting who we actually are. It's not depressing to concede that you won't ever get around to playing racquetball again after twenty years, or that you'll never finish that painting you started during the 1980s. (Yes, these are actually things my clients have gotten rid of.) Instead, it's loving to say to yourself that you're a wonderful, unique person just as you are, right now. When you find an item in the attic that you bought hoping one day you'd use it, remember that it was a stepping-stone to the person you are today. When you got it, you needed it. Even if you never used it once. Now you are ready to move on, because you've grown. Maturity is realizing we're all human and that wisdom comes from self-acceptance.

THE MAYBE PILE

To ease into things, I suggested to Jesse that we create a section of the house where we could put inherited items that we *might* get rid of. I called it the Maybe Pile—another secret weapon of mine. A Maybe Pile basically offers people some breathing room when the going gets a little too tough for them to make snap decisions about items. It's not kicking the can down the road: It's actually a subtle way to introduce into your head the idea of being separated from these items. Once an item goes into the Maybe Pile, it's easier to imagine yourself getting rid of it. And really, 75 percent of the stuff in Jesse and Maggie's place went into the Maybe Pile. It was easy for him to tell himself that he wasn't getting rid of the rolltop desk, the record player, the dishes, the dresser, or the clothes—he was just *considering* it by putting them into the Maybe Pile. Three weeks later, when the time came to empty the Maybe Pile, he found it much easier than he would have otherwise. With time, the idea of getting rid of those Maybe items had worked its way through Jesse's mind. In the end, only a handful of Maybes went into the Keep Pile. Time is the key ingredient of the Maybe Pile. With Maggie's encouragement and everyone listening to the stories attached to the objects, Jesse was able to let go.

The only things that remained in the Maybe Pile were things that Jesse put on his Legacy List.

LEGACY LIST

A Legacy List isn't just the catchy title of my hit show on PBS. A Legacy List—which I go into deeply in Step Five—is also a tally of five or six must-have keepsakes, items that have so much inherent worth that it just makes sense to hold on to them. They are the material possessions that you value the most. You will tell their stories for years to come. Preserving them for generations past and present can be a wonderful way of keeping your ancestors and loved ones alive. For all the importance of decluttering and downsizing—that's why you're reading this book, after all—it's crucial to set aside a few select things that you are going to keep. For one thing, preserving the past, savoring the special moments and people from your life, is a deeply human activity. You're trying to simplify and improve your life by paring down your possessions, not attempting to remove all traces of your past like Don Draper from *Mad Men*. Also, by allowing yourself to indulge in half a dozen essential artifacts, you'll have an easier time getting rid of the less important stuff. Telling myself I'll never eat mint chocolate chip ice cream again is not realistic; I can better stick to a diet where I have ice cream once a week (maybe twice).

For Jesse, the must-haves were these: one of his dad's old suits, his grandmother's crossword puzzle books, an end table, a china cabinet, and a hardback chair. As you can probably guess by now, I made sure to ask him why he wanted those items on his Legacy List: I wanted to hear his stories of these most valued objects. Truth be told, it would be hard for most people to understand preserving crossword puzzles that have already been solved. But all that mattered was that they were important to him. Sentimental value, like beauty, is in the eye of the beholder.

TAKING TIME TO CELEBRATE

Once you make some progress in your clutter, take a breather, kick up your feet, and enjoy the moment. You've worked hard to get here. After Jesse, Maggie, and I got through the table or finished a drawer or room, we cheered our success. Celebrate your accomplishments, no matter how small. I was constantly impressed by Jesse's bravery and emotional intelligence in going through his family's possessions, and I told him so. I've learned one truth over the years, both at home and at work: Praise inspires us, so pile on the verbal trophies, no matter how big or small the accomplishment! Don't underestimate this tip. Praise will keep the ball rolling and set the tone for success.

With one month of a little strategizing and a lot of hard work, we had their place spacious and tidy, ready for that baby to arrive. Jesse went from being unable to even start the process of decluttering to being a lean cleaning machine. He started making strategic choices about his objects that had seemed impossible for him to make just days and weeks earlier. He'd kept a few important things; the rest we tossed, donated, sold, or recycled. And yes, the baby was born healthy, and they eventually had a second kid. And a third. Now they have a new problem—too many children's toys cluttering the home! But that's a wonderful problem to have, familiar to any parent. (I often step on Legos going to the kitchen for coffee.)

People sometimes ask me how I decided on the strategies, tricks, and tips that I use when helping people rid themselves of the nonessential items from their overcrowded living spaces. It wasn't random and it definitely wasn't instinctive. It came about through working with people like Maggie and Jesse.

Left to our own devices, most of us will find a reason to keep everything. That's why knowing what to keep and acting on that knowledge with courage and boldness are some of the hardest parts of the process. But as you do the hard work, remember this: Preserving as much space as possible is essential not just to the appearance of a home but to its livability. Ask yourself, "What type of life do I want to lead? How will the object in my hands enhance that life?" Jesse needed to make space in his home not just for his baby but for his future. It was cluttered with remnants of his past. But rest assured: You never fully leave behind the people you once loved. They will always be part of your story. And you will always have the items and memories on your Legacy List.

And, as we'll see in the next chapter, the photographs and documents we choose to keep.

MATT'S TWELVE TIPS
FOR GETTING STARTED

- Begin with the Ten-Minute Sweep.
- Set a deadline.
- Understand your why.
- Choose a space that sets you up for success.
- Don't delay, start right away.
- Remember the one-month rule.
- Accept outside help.
- Give yourself permission to let go.
- Love who you actually are.
- Use a Maybe Pile strategically.
- Create a Legacy List.
- Take time to celebrate.

Sort Through Pictures and Documents

THE MOMENT I WALKED INTO Linda and Eric's home for an episode we were shooting of *Legacy List with Matt Paxton*, I knew I was somewhere special.

Both librarians and recent empty nesters, they were downsizing to a two-bedroom apartment from a gorgeous 1930s home on a tree-lined street near Rock Creek Park in Washington, D.C., where they'd lived for twenty-eight years. From my first glance in the foyer, I could see the house was a monument to African American history—which is to say that it was a monument to a vital part of American history. The photos adorning the walls were of celebrated heroes and ordinary people who committed heroic acts—all members of their families. One picture showcased Eric's uncle, a pianist who played with jazz legends Louis Armstrong and Jelly Roll Morton. In another picture, Linda's cousin looked spiffy in a suit next to a young Barack Obama. Eric's grandmother, who was black, and his grandfather, who was white, looked out at me from a framed photograph in the living room.

"Interracial relationships occurred more often throughout history than we know," Linda said when she noticed me looking at the photo. That meant the picture was important not just to her family; it was a peek into America's past. The couple had many pictures like that, on the walls and in well-organized photo albums. The photos were living artifacts of their family's remarkable experience as well as the country's history.

And then there were the documents. As you might expect from two people with degrees in library sciences, Linda and Eric and had done a monumental job of organizing their families' paperwork. Linda's father had been a pioneering plumber in the federal government. She showed me boxes of awards, certificates, newspaper clippings, and handwritten notes documenting his achievements. She had once been charged with cleaning out her aunt's house, from which she inherited more documents. She became an expert in "telling the stories of the ancestors," she told me, and also "in being careful when you're cleaning out and cleaning up." I don't normally praise people for saving a lot of stuff, but I was amazed at the trove of history that Linda and Eric had devoted themselves to maintaining. And all these papers were organized to share that history with their kids and, eventually, grandkids.

As I walked through their home, I saw that it was already junk-free. Indeed, Linda and Eric had already done the work of packaging, cleaning, and sorting most of their items in preparation for the moving trucks that would be arriving in a few days. So what did they need from me?

Linda explained that they were down to the photos and papers and needed my guidance in figuring out what among their treasure trove of history to leave behind. I found it remarkable that even these experts in safeguarding precious legacies were stuck knowing what to bring in a move. If they have trouble, no wonder the rest of us do, too!

I had long seen that people have immense difficulty letting go of photographs and documents. More than any other items, these are the toughest to sort through. Sometimes people want to keep all their pictures and papers; other times, folks want to get rid of everything but worry about accidentally discarding something important or valuable.

What I do is help people find something in the middle, preserving the past while clearing out the way—and the space—to create new memories. In this chapter, first we'll go through the photos, then the documents. We'll talk about mostly about paper, but I'll walk you through the magic of digital solutions as well.

· · ·

When I met Linda and Eric, they had already prepared their Legacy List. At the top was that famous "four-generation photograph," which showed four women in Linda's family, one of whom was formerly enslaved. Another legacy item showcased Eric's father, a Coast Guard member on the first ship that was racially integrated. The pictures were incredible. Linda and Eric were unique in having so many trailblazers on both sides of their family, but most of us have generations' worth of photographs, including collections we have inherited from other family members. I can firmly say this after decades of helping thousands of people declutter, downsize, and move: Pictures are frequently the items that most hold us back.

WHY PHOTOS ARE SO POWERFUL

Digital images may be the norm today, but most of my clients have tons of physical photos, too—posted on walls; piled in boxes and bags; stuffed in albums; tucked into drawers; forgotten in closets, attics, and basements. Choosing the few keepers from among these pictures is the next step on your journey.

These small, faded, sometimes grainy pieces of paper stimulate powerful emotions in us. Those images are potent reminders of the past, containing some of the best stories of our lives. They capture reality in a way unmatched by any other items except for maybe journals or home videos. People often inherit more photos from previous generations than any other heirlooms, and we feel obligated to hold on to them.

It's not just pictures of loved ones, vacations, birthdays, and weddings that are hard to part with. I've seen people alarmed at the idea of tossing out photos of such random things as garbage cans, staplers, and even bags of chicken feed (that last one reminded a client of the farm he grew up on). Sometimes the pictures are actually of negative people and experiences, such as scorned ex-boyfriends and ex-husbands, warfighting, or items that have been stolen.

Sometimes we feel that in throwing away photos, we're throwing away our past—which, in a way, we are. The hardest of all might be the pictures that reveal to us opportunities we didn't take, paths we didn't go down, options we rejected. Saying goodbye to those pictures is yet another reminder of those forgone lives we might have lived. We have the nagging feeling that the photos *may* be important, somehow, even if they're not. It doesn't matter if the photos are of good or poor quality, either. They are the clearest depiction of our past, visibly reflecting our triumphs and tragedies. That's what makes junking photos so difficult.

So let's go back to Linda and Eric's photo collection and figure out how to sift through it. I saw that while the pictures on the walls and framed on display were vital, they also had many that were less important. They had hundreds of shots of weddings, vacations, high school and college graduation ceremonies, baby namings—not to mention the many pictures from Christmases, Thanksgivings, and Fourth of July get-togethers. For many of the snaps of these celebrations, they had doubles. Like many people, Linda and Eric even held on to blurry or poorly staged photos, where people were half out of the shots. Some photos were in albums. Some had stamped dates on the front, and others had notations of dates, people, and events on the back. Others held no clue as to who was in the shot or when it was taken. Still others were in shoeboxes or drawers. Even these professional archivists couldn't catalog all the pictures they had!

VISUAL STORIES

The first thing I did was collect all their photos and lay them on the floor of the den. Eric and Linda saw their lives, and the lives of their family, spread out before them. Separating themselves from that seemed, understandably, challenging. But the finish line was a fact: They simply could not take all the pictures with them, because they didn't have enough space.

"Remember why we are doing our work," I reminded them. "The pictures are inhibiting you from moving. So they're not bringing value to your life; they're actually taking away from your quality of life." The truth is that unless you're a professional photographer, our photos are just pieces of paper. They're only valuable because of the meaning our stories bring to them. Without understanding the significance behind them, there's no meaning. Would you look twice at the famous photo of the Beatles walking across a random street if you didn't know John, Paul, George, and Ringo? A shot of a white-haired man riding his bicycle or sticking his tongue out is thrilling only because the man, Einstein, is synonymous with scientific genius. The same is true of the photos from our personal lives. The snapshot of that teenager matters because she grew into the woman who gave birth to us.

What that means, though, is that if we find a way to keep the powerful emotions and memories we associate with the pictures, the pictures themselves are less important. The stories the pictures tell are what matters. *So tell those stories.* Take the time to enjoy your pictures by relaying their meaning to someone, preferably someone for whom the photos have meaning, too. If you're worried those stories won't get passed on to future generations, talk into an audio recorder as though you're speaking directly to your future great-great-grandchildren. Most phones now have an app for recording audio.

HANDLING THE PHOTOS

One of the first things I learned about handling pictures is that you need to wear cotton gloves. That's especially true with older photos, but it's wise for any pictures that you're handling. Wearing the gloves protects the photos from fingerprints as well as the natural oils and acids on our skin that can break down and damage pictures over time. And please, don't eat or drink while you're going through the pictures. I usually have a bottle of water by my side, but I move it when I'm culling through pictures.

LOSE THE BULK FIRST

Take the pictures out of their frames. Discard or donate any frames you aren't currently using. If you decide down the road that you want to replace these bulky items, they are inexpensive.

The next and deeply gratifying next step is to toss the duplicates. Most of the pictures you have, you don't even need one—you definitely don't need two! Trust me, you only need one shot of your cousin falling into a swimming pool.

Next, toss anything blurry. Unless it's a modern piece of art, nothing blurry belongs in your home. Also, throw out photos of generic landscapes, such as beaches, mountains, and bodies of water, unless you're a professional photographer and can sell them for lots of money. The world has plenty of these photos!

After that, let's tackle a category some people have trouble with: pictures of people you don't know. That includes old pictures, photos of long-lost family members, and childhood friends. Out they go. Remember, you still have their stories. Those few of my readers active in genealogy have my permission to save a few more of the family pictures of people you don't recognize. The rest of us have no excuses.

MAKING THE HARDER CHOICES

Once we thinned out the bulk a little, Linda and Eric faced more difficult choices. Most of the photos that remained in their collection were at least decent-quality shots of people they could identify. Note that few of us are actually in the same boat as Linda and Eric, who have a long family tradition of breaking barriers to make history. But even they found ways to downsize their collection. I used a tip from my photography expert friend Cathi Nelson—you'll hear more about her in a second—who calls it the 80/20 rule. I told Linda and Eric, "You're going to discard 80 percent of your photos, and you're allowed to preserve at most 20 percent of them." This simple breakdown is easy to remember and will help you arrive at a manageable collection. Being the decluttering advocate that I am, I generally recommend going 90/10. I normally tell people to, for those photos you absolutely *must* keep in print, keep only enough to fill the equivalent of two shoeboxes. You want to be able to carry all your photos with you in your arms—no more than that. But Linda and Eric were in an exceptional situation, wanting to preserve their photos not just because they were of family members but because they were unique contributions to U.S. history. For them, Cathi's 80/20 rule made a lot of sense, I thought.

As we worked together, however, they managed to exceed the 80/20 target. They realized that the pictures they actually wanted to keep were only the photos of undeniable historic value, and about one-tenth of their family ones. For each of those snaps, we confirmed that we had all the relevant information about the location, date, individuals, and meaning. Linda and Eric were mostly hanging on to the rest of the shots because they didn't know what else to do with them. Their family record was exceptional in its civic value—but no matter your situation, photos of families are what you should prioritize. Some people wonder if their lives will even be interesting to their kids, grandkids, great-grandkids, and other descendants down the line. The answer is: absolutely! It's not a question of if but when people who come after us will want to learn about us. "Every human being on the planet is interested in where they came from," Cathi says. But they won't be interested in *all* your photos. Those shots you took of the Grand Canyon? Everyone's photos of the Grand Canyon will look pretty much the same.

Similarly, remember that, for the most part, most of us do not need to keep the majority of our pictures. With Facebook or an average genealogy website like Ancestry.com, you can find virtually anyone now. Plus, you aren't required to single-handedly document seven generations back of family history. Unless you have photos dating to the mid-1800s, they almost certainly won't be placed in a museum or be of interest to scholars. It does take courage to throw out photos—indeed, to throw out anything you've been hanging on to for a long time—but it's a step you should encourage yourself to take. Watching Linda and Eric make the hard choices was a bit nerve-racking, even for me. But it was gratifying because we knew we were checking all the boxes and doing the right thing, picture by picture.

Although I was able to offer Linda and Eric guidance, I should admit up front that I'm not a natural photography expert. I'm a guy who thinks cell phones get the job done for my photos, and before that I had a simple point-and-shoot camera. But for the last ten years, clients have been asking me on an almost daily basis what to do with their pictures. Whether I'm teaching a class, giving a speech, or helping a family on a television show, the most frequent question I get is about pics. So after getting asked about it one too many times, I reached out to a leader in the industry.

PHOTO MANAGERS

Cathi Nelson, who I mentioned earlier, got into scrapbooking in the 1980s, when organizing personal photos into workbooks to tell life stories became a major craze. She had adopted a son and wanted him one day to see the moments when he became a part of his family. Cathi and her husband didn't know anything about the origins of the child they were making a part of their lives—not where he came from, who his birth family members were, or how he came to be given up for adoption.

When the time came, Cathi got priceless shots of him entering her arms and being carried into his new home for the first time, and she captured other unforgettable, intimate moments. After pasting them onto blank paper, she wrote details about the moments next to the photos: the relevant dates, names, locations, and meaning. Those details are crucial, she says, and many are conspicuously absent from the thousands of digital photos many of us carry around on our phones. Those missing details are a huge problem for anyone wanting to make use of these pictures—I'll explain why in a minute.

Through her devotion to scrapbooking, Cathi developed

skills that became badly needed when the digital era began. "As Baby Boomers got older, people felt overwhelmed when they realized they had a lifetime of photos," she says. Enter her organization, The Photo Managers, which bills itself as "a community of professionals who are passionate about helping their clients manage photo collections and tell their stories." Having worked with her photo managers for a long time, I can attest to the accuracy of their self-description. They're all like Cathi: people who know how to turn the visual evidence of your life story into something memorable to last for generations.

I've found the Photo Managers are to photo management and organizing what NASMM and NAPO are to move management—the best in the business. Notably, this organization, too, was started by a woman who filled a niche in the market after seeing there was nobody else doing what she needed done in her own life. (All across my line of work, in fact, I see this same pattern: It's women of every age leading the way forward, innovating and clearing the path to better ways of doing things. This middle-aged father of seven is lucky to just be along for the ride!)

When Should You Opt for a Photo Manager?

Maybe you don't know where to start with the dozens of boxes of photos that were accumulated over decades and have been collecting dust in your closet. You wouldn't be alone—I have seen people with entire rooms in their homes packed with photos. Linda and Eric were unusual in having photos of undeniable historical importance, but they were typical in the amount they'd amassed. If you just have too many photos to handle the job on your own, you should consider a photo manager. Cathi's group, The Photo Managers, provides certification and accreditation to its members, which is crucial because it means they have a body of knowledge and hands-on experience to enable them to meet every need. You can find a photo manager either through that group or punch the words "photo managers near me" into a search engine online. They'll do all the time-consuming, labor-intensive work for you: sort your photographs, scan them, upload them to the internet, organize them in an eye-pleasing and logical manner, and store them for you in the cloud (online storage) or on your computer.

The Digital Era

Never forget that we are living in the digital revolution, I told Linda and Eric. (If I ever forget by, say, reading a print newspaper, my kids call me a dinosaur.) Digitization is *the* ultimate solution to your photo problem. This was my top suggestion to Linda and Eric, and it's my top suggestion to you: Digitize every photo you care about. Even the ones you definitely are keeping—it's not enough just to keep the print. Actually, you should *especially* digitize the ones you are keeping, since those are your most valued shots, and you could one day lose them. If you didn't digitize your pictures and woke up one day to discover that, heaven forbid, there was a fire or other natural disaster in your home, or your possessions were stolen, you will regret not listening to ol' Matt Paxton.

I showed Linda and Eric how we could simply take a photo of their photos with their phones, or scan them with an affordable scanning device, and upload them to their computers, a hard drive, or the cloud. Then the photos exist safely forever. The easy accessibility of scanners and cheap hard drive space has progressed tremendously recently; it wasn't as advanced even when I was working with Linda and Eric, just a few short years ago. The technology will surely continue to progress in the coming years, making it ever easier to safeguard any snaps you want to be sure never to lose.

But you must take the time to actually write the stories down and document who is in these pictures, or you will have the same problem as having hundreds of boxes of pictures that are physically in your home. A big digital pile of pictures with no organization is still a big pile of pictures with no meaning. I've had many families over the years tell me that they wish they had written down their parents' stories—sometimes the parents had meant to do so but never got around to it. Now all that remains of those stories are photographs that are unexplainable to younger generations because they lack the indispensable details that provide context.

If you're a child of the digital era, you might have thousands of pictures scattered across multiple desktop computers, laptops, phones, hard drives, thumb drives, social media, and other platforms and devices. That's wonderful for documenting your life, but it's terrible for having that documentation organized! It's worth nothing that when you take a picture on your phone, it's easy to enable GPS and artificial intelligence functioning to capture the date and location of the contents of the photo. Young people, or us not-so-young people addicted to our handheld devices, might wonder what we're missing by snapping countless pictures without adding additional details. Well, when Cathi's son got older, he wanted to know about his birth circumstances, as many adopted children do. Through an ancestry DNA website, they were able to track down his first cousin. And so, as caught on camera in a priceless photograph, Cathi's son met a birth-family member for the first time in his life. It was an incredible moment. But as Cathi astutely points out, unless they wrote down the particular significance of that meeting on the back of the photo, future generations would be unable to understand its momentousness. It would just look to them like two people shaking hands. *That* is why detailing your pictures matters, and why having a hundred thousand photos just clutters your life unhelpfully, even if they're just on your phone. (It's also why you should delete most pictures from your phone right away.)

Full disclosure: I get so many questions about digital organization that I started my own photo digitization company, called Memories by Matt Paxton (MemoriesByMattPaxton.com). More photo ideas can be found in the Resources section at the back of this book.

How a Photo Manager Helps

Linda and Eric had a good number of rare pictures—and they were rightly concerned about the pictures' preservation for posterity—so we tapped a photo manager we found on Cathi's website. A photo manager can work with you to create virtual scrapbooks or organize your print ones. In our case, we wanted someone to walk us through the possibilities for displaying the photos online in a way that was easy to understand, was accessible to family members across the country, and would serve as a living project that Linda and Eric could add details and newly discovered facts onto.

Here are some services the photo manager offered to us:

- **Work around the chronology issue.** Our photo manager told us that many people worry that their giant collection of pictures cannot be organized well digitally because they are undated and out of chronological order. That's not a problem. "We can organize around theme," Cathi says. For example, our photo manager helped us sort the pictures according to family celebrations. In lining up, displaying, and explaining the history of Linda and Eric's children's birthday parties, it was unimportant whether the shot of their fifteenth birthday preceded the sixteenth or vice versa. What mattered instead is that family members were present. If you're trying to demonstrate the passage of time through the years, drastic changes are easy to recognize without exact dates.

- **Set up backup systems.** I can't emphasize how important this rule is: If you digitize *anything*, you'll want to back it up. Don't just keep your important photographs and documents on your computer—this is a recipe for disaster. If your computer crashes, gets lost or stolen, or contracts a virus, everything on there can be lost. This is the first thing Cathi told me, and she preaches it every single time I hear her speak. "Back up your backup."

- **Design digital photo books and slideshows.** Print photos can also be produced as part of handsome scrapbooks.

But I recommend this option only if you commit to reducing your collection so your photos can fit into one or two books. If you turn your unwieldy photo collection into an unwieldy book collection, you've just created a new, bulkier problem for yourself. We're supposed to be downsizing here, people!

- **Consider** the endless possibilities for displaying pictures digitally. Our photo manager showed us how we could:

  - **Use a digital frame** (there are many available online) or your smart TV to display your favorite pictures.
  - **Create an entire website** to tell a family's story.
  - **Design eye-popping slideshows.**
  - **Edit and restore the images.** Using special technology, photo managers can take an aging, disintegrating shot of your grandmother and make it look like it was taken today—in vibrant colors.
  - **Select and employ the best storage system.** Apple, Amazon, and Google are the most popular, but they are good only for storage, Cathi says, not for displaying your pictures. To make them become something that people actually will want to look at, she suggests opting for Forever.com or SmugMug.com.

THE BEGINNING OF THE END

With my help—okay, it was mostly because of Cathi's advice and our photo manager's tireless work—Linda and Eric were able to narrow down their collection to the bare essentials. That meant digitizing all their photos and concentrating on the best shots of immediate family as well as on the photos handed down to them from previous generations. "I need these for my grandkids," Linda told me. She didn't even have grandkids yet! But that's how attached she was to pictures. I could hardly discourage her—she had one legendary picture of women studying home economics in the 1920s at Howard University, the distinguished historically black college. The ladies in the photograph looked as glamorous and sophisticated as movie stars. This shot was taken at a time of horrific violence and discrimination against African Americans, forty years before the civil rights movement—amassing all that elegance in one room in the 1920s was a statement of humanity. The best part of working with Linda and Eric was learning the amazing history of dozens of snapshots in their collection. That's the only way they were able to even think about letting go of most of their prints. I know they were glad they did and felt a great relief at having a more manageable collection of photos, one that was usable and enjoyable for them because it was small enough for them to look at in one sitting.

PREVENTING FUTURE PHOTO CLUTTER

Once Linda and Eric completed the painstaking work of narrowing down their photos to a lovely, usable archive, I warned them about something I've seen with numerous clients: They could fall back into the same problematic habits that led them to call me in the first place, especially since our phones allow us to take snapshots so easily. Luckily, however, technology offers a way around this problem. My phone has an app that allows me to automatically send the photos and videos I record directly to my mother's smart TV, in her home. It's an incredible way to keep my mother updated on the stories of our lives. She often goes to her smart TV to see the cool new pictures we have sent. My children don't remember life without this gadget, so they often remind me: "Don't forget to send that pic to Grandma's TV." This app provides an alternative to the cumbersome and bulky process of printing out the shots, framing them, and sending them to loved ones.

WHAT TO DO ABOUT PAPERS

Linda and Eric were having trouble going separate ways with items beyond photos, however. Equally difficult was the assemblage of documents that were in eight or nine boxes and one full filing cabinet, and on several shelves (albeit stacked neatly). There were precious papers documenting African American history, as well as personal family papers dealing with finances and legal matters.

I had never seen the type of boxes housing the papers. "They're special boxes," Eric explained. The boxes were acid-free, which meant that they could hold documents for long periods—decades, even centuries—without decaying. Some of the boxes were tucked away in the basement, which was dark and damp. Linda told me about the importance of keeping delicate documents in a cool space. "If they're in the sun, they can fade," she told me. Linda knew her stuff: If you have a basement, store your vital papers there. Never in the attic or garage, where weather changes can affect your papers and pictures. If your basement is prone to flooding, make sure the boxes are on a high shelf. If you have valuable documents that can't be kept in a basement (or you don't have a basement), ask the local storage place for specific climate-controlled areas. Almost all of them have those units, and they will cost just a bit more than the outside units. If you've gotten this far, you know that I rarely recommend renting storage spaces, but one exception is for documents of significant importance. Those are worth shelling out some cash to protect.

History aside, Linda and Eric needed to hold on to some crucial papers in their stacks: financial documents, insurance records, legal matters, and a will. Whatever your situation, you're always going to want to keep some other vital documents, too: birth and death certificates, housing documents, contracts, tax returns, employment information, and so on. It's tempting, when looking at intimidating stacks of paper with fine print, to just opt to hold on to all of it, lest you accidentally discard something important. But if you keep all the papers, you're unable to quickly find the necessary documents when you need them, in addition to retaining the mess that's clogging your living space—and life. Sometimes people don't even know which papers they have because they're mixed in with stacks of useless other documents. Better to sort through it all now. Everything can and should be digitized. Still, there are a few special items for which you'll want to keep original copies. You can use this list as a skeleton key.

Matt's List of Important Original Documents to Keep—Permanently

- Social Security cards
- Copy of driver's licenses
- Passports, current and past
- Naturalization or immigration papers
- Voter ID cards
- Birth certificates
- Death certificates
- Marriage certificates
- Workers' compensation forms
- Immunization records (including your COVID-19 vaccination card)
- Divorce decrees
- Adoption papers
- Alimony settlement agreements
- Annulment decrees or settlements
- Change-of-name certificates
- Cohabitation agreements
- Prenuptial and postnuptial agreements
- Qualified domestic relations orders
- Car titles

- Land contracts
- Copyrights
- Patents and trademarks
- Property settlement agreements
- Wills
- Living wills
- Trust documents
- Powers of attorney (health and financial)
- Medicare cards
- Military records, especially (but not only) regarding financial benefits
- Mortgages, home deeds, or leases
- Pension plans
- Retirement plans registration (old statements can be discarded)
- Business licenses
- Insurance policies
- Stock certificates

Okay, so those are the few documents that you never want to throw out. Scan them, digitize them, but also save them. Then there are the things you'll want to hold on to for a while, even as you scan and digitize them. Remember, back up your backup.

Matt's List of Important Documents to Keep—Temporarily

- Tax records (seven years)
- Legal records (five years after a case is closed)
- Medical records (up to two years after full payment in case of disputes)
- Outstanding loans (until paid off)

THE FIVE-MINUTE TIME CAPSULE

I recommend to my clients that they build a small time capsule of some information they need to have at their fingertips, for themselves or their family, should something happen to them. It'll take you just five minutes to put together. All you need is a pen and paper—or a computer and printer—and some information.

- Write down the date, account numbers, institution, agent, contact information, and approximate amounts contained in your:

- Checking, savings, and investment accounts
- Life insurance policies

- Write down your:

  - Phone number

  - All medications, including prescription information and names and phone numbers of doctors and pharmacies
  - Login information and passwords for critical websites, including:
    - Email
    - Social media accounts, such as Facebook, Twitter, and Instagram. Believe it or not, these are important to have when you need to shut the account down if someone has passed away unexpectedly, or if your accounts are hacked.
    - Banks and other financial institutions
    - Subscriptions to magazines, newspapers, and delivery services

Once you have those jotted down, place them in an unmarked bag or large envelope. Keeping the documents together in a designated, discreet spot is a quick way to always have vital information when you need it. I strongly recommend a small personal safe.

A great resource for pulling together all your vital information is AARP's *Checklist for My Family: A Guide to My History, Financial Plans, and Final Wishes*, available wherever books are sold.

SAFE-TY FIRST

You'll want to lock all these documents somewhere safe—in a safe, in fact. Safes now are inexpensive, secure, and unlocked with fingerprint scans, not with keys, padlocks, or dials. You won't have to worry about forgetting the combination or losing the keys. Safes can be purchased for less than $150 at your local home improvement store or online. It'll be some of the best money you'll ever spend.

THE SHREDDING SOLUTION

Linda and Eric also had lots of paper that *wasn't* precious: old tax records and bills, receipts, statements dating back years, letters, notebooks, manuals for appliances they no longer owned,

WHAT TO DO IF YOU FIND A PAPER STOCK CERTIFICATE

Some of my readers will be too young to even know what stock certificates are. I often find them hidden throughout homes that I clean out. They are live, active financial instruments, claims to real cash. In 2001, the New York Stock Exchange eliminated the need for paper stock certificates and converted to the digital tracking system that is used today. I have been finding old stock certificates in homes for years. Sometimes they have already been converted digitally, and sometimes they have not. Once I helped a client unearth a few stock certificates worth more than $2 million in an envelope marked "trash." I've also found stock certificates that had zero value. But even some of the zero-

cards, and much else. They knew that most of this stuff, if not all of it, should go. But they were worried about someone finding valuable information by rummaging through their garbage. So they kept all of it. It's a common fallback strategy. I told them that I had an easy solution to recycling their paperwork safely: Shred it all.

You can pick up a decent shredder for less than $50 from any office supply store. Experts recommend a security microcut shredder, which cuts paper into confetti. As with a safe, a shred-

value certificates, because they are beautiful documents, have value on the collectors' market as art. You'll have to do the research to find out.

If you have an old stock certificate, look for the tracking number—called a CUSIP number—on the front. You can search the CUSIP number on many financial websites by using their "Find Symbol" tool. But don't just take the internet's word for it; reach out to an investment professional for confirmation. Especially if these certificates are a part of an estate, you may want to hire a professional to handle this for you since, depending upon the state where they were issued or found, there could be complicated tax implications. The cost of the professional could far outweigh the tax savings of handling it incorrectly.

der is something you should have in your home to secure all your information. If you don't want that option, you can haul your paper to a free shredding service offered by many local governments and businesses. If you're having difficulty finding one, Office Depot or similar stores offer low-cost shredding services. Some people keep a cardboard box in the trunk of their car and place the documents to be shredded in that box. I recommend that method because, once the box is full, you just drive it to a store or a free shredding location and let someone else lift it out of the trunk. Then you never have big boxes in your home, you don't hurt your back lifting heavy boxes, and you remember to get your documents shredded more frequently because they're in your trunk.

For massive amounts of paper, you might want to outsource the job instead of spending loads of time shredding your own. In that case, professional shredders will handle the task. With mobile shredders, they'll come to your home and pick up your documents. For others, you'll have to drop off your documents or ship them.

Whichever shredding choice you make, it's a service well worth investing in. Identity theft is rampant. Thieves literally search in garbage dumps for discarded paper that contains valuable data such as Social Security numbers and medical records. Trust me on this: It's far better to shell out a few hundred dollars now to protect yourself than to spend endless time, patience, and energy reclaiming your identity.

Linda and Eric understood my logic, even though they probably wanted to throw me in the Potomac River when I told them they needed to spend money to shred old papers. But over the next few days, we accomplished it. And when the movers came, I was able to send Linda and Eric off with only the documents and photos they decided they needed to keep. Even considering their family's devotion to chronicling the past, they were able to recycle bins of paper and digitize most of the past, the better to prepare for the future.

Ultimately, that's what my work is about—leaving the past behind in an emotionally satisfying way to step boldly into the future. People tend to tell me the items they want to bring with them in a move—or talk about agonizing over what to bring—instead of telling me the life they want to live where they are going. But you live your best life when you understand that what really matters is not possessions but memories, and a lot of those memories are stored in documents and pictures. That's why turning an item into a legacy is crucial. We'll talk about that in the next chapter.

. . . .

Decide What to Keep and Build Your Legacy List

NICOLE AND NEIL ARE SOME of my oldest friends. In high school, everyone had a crush on Nicole, including Neil and maybe even me. She was smart, funny, and beautiful, the third generation of a family of Greek immigrants who built a thriving dry-cleaning business. She eventually married Neil and they had two kids.

In 2014, Nicole phoned me with the sad news that her grandfather had passed away—her grandmother had predeceased him—and she needed my help cleaning out their home. Her parents lived across the country, and she was the oldest daughter, so the job fell to her. Yes, it's an honor, but it's also a ton of work that is usually too much for one person. Nicole was taking on the job of all three generations of this close-knit extended family. She wanted to get it right.

I arrived at what must have been the most amazing house in Richmond. I knew that Nicole's grandparents had been successful, sure, but this home was filled with paintings by famous local artists, replicas of ancient Greek sculptures, marble floors, expensive chandeliers, high-end midcentury modern furniture, and fancy rugs. Around town, her grandparents were never flashy; they drove used cars and wore inexpensive clothing. So I'd never realized just how well-off they were.

Nicole had no idea what to keep from her family's possessions. The paintings? Her grandfather's stamp collection? Her grandmother's jewelry?

"I'm not sure what they'd *want* me to have," she told me. Her grandparents' will detailed what to do with the biggest items—the business, cars, and home—but was silent on most other things that remained in their home. Because her grandparents had so much stuff, deciding what to keep was proving to be excruciating for her. Nicole was lost.

Although the will was inadequate, Nicole's grandparents had left her with something more valuable: a lifetime of good memories. As first-generation immigrants, Nicole's grandparents had radically different experiences than she did, which she had loved hearing about. We walked around the house where she'd spent so much time as a grandchild who always knew she was loved. She talked about her memories, and we worked together to find options to help her decide what to keep.

It's vital to reduce the stockpile of your belongings, as we've seen from previous chapters. But how do you know what to hold on to? Figuring that out is the next step on your journey, and for that, I'll rely on what I've learned from my TV show, *Legacy List with Matt Paxton*. And look, I'm now living a minimalist lifestyle, and I'm married to another (much better-looking) minimalist. I believe life is generally fullest when our material possessions are fewest. But I'm a *selective* minimalist, because there is an exception to my rule against holding on to stuff. And the exception is for what I call Legacy List items.

I named my show *Legacy List with Matt Paxton* for a reason: Establishing and passing on a legacy of memory-packed items is a way of keeping ourselves and loved ones alive when we're apart. What you'll need to do here is change your mindset from one of getting rid of stuff to selecting the few Legacy List items that will enhance your life today and best relay who you are to the next generation. Ask yourself, "What are the items that will help me live happily and keep my story living on forever?" I know that's not an easy shift, but it's indispensable. The idea of a Legacy List can be your guiding star to help you know what to retain while you're decluttering, downsizing, and moving. Let me tell how Nicole thrived with this strategy—and how it can work for you.

BUILDING A LEGACY

Nicole and Neil weren't a wealthy couple: Nicole was a midlevel executive and Neil was a stonemason. But they were satisfied with what they had. Their happiness focused on experiences with their family and not with stuff.

Going through her grandparents' home, Nicole told me, "Neil and I don't need anything." We had to find a different framework to decide what to keep.

I suggested that she create a Legacy List. That involves asking yourself, "What kind of legacy do I want to pass on?" What are the stories about you and your loved ones that you want to be told years down the road? A great legacy item is one that helps keep people and their memories alive, long after they're gone from our lives. Remember that an item's value lies not in the item itself—the item is just the vehicle for remembering someone you love and how they made you feel. That's why good legacy items are rarely the most financially valuable items. They're ones that are *emotionally* valuable. Your choices should echo this understanding.

In response to the question, Nicole walked me through their home, showing me the many reminders of the life her grandparents left behind in Greece. They had a *briki,* a Greek coffee pot that brewed scents she'd never forget. They had a Greek backgammon game called Tavli; she picked up the game pieces, fondly remembering playing with her grandmother. She showed me textiles and pottery in colors I'd never seen before. "How can I choose just a few items and let go of *any* of this?" she asked agonizingly.

"I know what you're struggling with," I said. "Let me tell you about *my* family's legacy items."

Paxton Family Legacy Items

In the introduction, I told you about my father dying. What I didn't mention is that my dad, stepdad, and two grandfathers died within a two-year period. I was heartbroken. Even worse, I was tasked with clearing out their homes (four in total), going through their stuff, and exploring their stories. It fell to me to sort through their businesses, their souvenirs from World War II, the minutiae from their hobbies. The garages were the hardest for me. They had letters from military buddies, and I would sift through collections of tools these men had used to build their homes and their lives. Holding a hammer or drill in my hands, I would sit and think of the men who taught me to be the man I wanted to be, the man I *should* be. In a short period, I had to figure out how to keep the memories of these men alive—not just for me but for the kids I eventually wanted to have. My children would never know their grandfathers or great-grandfathers. My stories and whatever possessions of theirs I kept would be the only glimpse my kids got of the men who raised me.

The word "value" took on a new meaning. Unlike with Nicole's situation, none of my parents' and grandparents' possessions were worth much money. My family was never well-off, and the few expensive items they did own, like cars, depreciate in value and cost more to keep alive and maintain than they are worth. But cheap stuff? My family had lots of that! Buying cheap crap seemed to be my father's favorite thing to do. He couldn't resist inexpensive electronics, plastic kitchenware, or secondhand clothing. But I didn't need that stuff, and I didn't have room for it in my small apartment anyway. That's how I came up with the Legacy List idea.

My father was in advertising, so we cycled through being rich and broke a few times in our lives. One year when business wasn't so good, my dad convinced Tiffany's—yes, *the* Tiffany & Co.—to let him design its catalog. He was broke and living in an apartment, which he converted into a photography studio for the job. He designed and wrote the entire catalog himself. It was a smashing success and got his business back on track. When it came time to get paid, my dad worked out a trade for a ring he really liked instead of a badly needed cash payment. This ring was my dad living in his fantasy self—he was living in excess, but also with a dream. All of that wrapped up in a small gold ring, the original Legacy List item and the beginning of the core principle of my career helping families.

From my stepdad, I kept his car's license plate, VIZUN, which represented his devotion to his career and his mindset. As a young entrepreneur, that car and the license plate kept me motivated. I opted for my grandfather's fishing scale, which represented to me his incredible work ethic. When my siblings and I stayed at my granddad's ranch in the summer, he didn't allow us to go fishing on Fridays until all of our weekly chores on his farm were done. Maybe my most original idea was to take my great-aunt's trolley tokens. In her day, you'd drop in a token to get on Richmond trolleys. And until the end of her life, she hung on to a roll of those tokens, long after the trolleys had been replaced by buses and tokens had been replaced by cash and cash cards. She kept saying that she'd read somewhere that the tokens would return one day and by gosh she'd be sitting pretty with her stash! I always found that hilariously endearing and illustrative of her working-class life. Well, when I got married, I turned those tokens into cuff links for me and my groomsmen to wear. My wedding party loved hearing the story of my great-aunt's life. And when my kids are older, I'll show them those cuff links and share that same story.

I am grateful I held on to those Legacy List items I chose twenty years ago. They remind me of my family members intimately, although to outsiders they might seem like almost random objects.

Identifying the Legacy

I could almost see the light bulbs going off in Nicole's head when I talked about my family's legacy items. I asked her what she had loved best about her grandparents.

"They're the reason I'm here," she told me. She didn't mean they were the reason she was alive or sitting where we were—she meant that they were the reason she was in America. She told me they had made the brave decision to leave behind their families and uproot their lives in Greece, riding on ships through rough waters to the United States, all in the hope of living in freedom and giving their kids a chance for better lives. Once they settled in Virginia, Nicole continued, they scrimped and saved to open their own business. Despite not being native English speakers, they had, through sweat and entrepreneurialism, built a thriving business. "They lived the American dream," she said, her eyes tearing up. Nicole spent time in her childhood at those dry-cleaning shops, watching her family work. She heard her parents talk about *their* childhood memories in those shops, too.

I asked Nicole what she wanted her young kids to know about her grandparents. She thought about it for a minute, then responded:

"Their courage in coming here. Their selflessness. And their work ethic. It made their lives possible."

We had our starting point.

Discovering Your Legacy

Unlike Nicole, you might not know all the intricate details about your family. That's not uncommon. Previous generations didn't always share the intimate parts of their lives. I often hear of fathers and grandfathers who fought in wars overseas but never talked about their military experiences. So I recommend you sit down with your loved ones and ask them questions, recording the conversations. Here are just a few of my favorite conversation starters that I've learned over the years working with families in their homes. I would ask these questions just to break the silence and get the stories flowing. I doubt you'll get past the third question, because once people finally start revealing their lives, they realize the joy of doing so and have trouble stopping!

1. Where did you grow up, how long did you live there, and what did it look like?
2. What did you do for fun in high school?
3. What was the first job you got paid for, and how much did you get paid?
4. Tell me about your childhood best friend and your best memory of them.
5. What was your first car?
6. Who was your first love?
7. What is your favorite place you have ever visited? Who were you with, and how did you get there?
8. Who or what inspires you?
9. What is the most challenging thing you have ever accomplished, and why was it so difficult?
10. What is the one thing you want everyone to know about you when you are gone?

You may be the last person who has access to this knowledge, so don't be shy. It's your responsibility to document the stories, to tell them, to make sure someone knows about who these people are and how they lived their lives. If you don't, these memories may be lost forever. If you need help, don't hesitate to ask for it from your family members and friends.

WHO WANTS YOUR STUFF?

"Brutal honesty" is a phrase my clients often hear me use. Being brutally honest is a skill that I've used most of my life, sometimes to my detriment. But brutal honesty has been truly important when helping people discuss their family's possessions. That's because you need to decide who would want—and not want—your stuff.

Because Nicole's grandparents' will didn't cover everything, that question now loomed for Nicole. If only her grandparents were there one last time to guide her. She would have relished sitting down with them and discussing all that she felt for them—and which items would help her best tap into those emotions. She wondered why they didn't leave more detail in the will.

"Maybe they didn't think you'd want any of their stuff," I said. Her eyes widened. I'd guessed correctly. Nicole's grandparents had been modest people who couldn't imagine that their offspring would want their possessions.

A lot of people—some of you reading this right now—have the misconception that nobody wants your stuff. Countless people over the years have told me, "My kids don't really care about anything I have." I'm sure it may seem true—after all, we don't as a rule invite family members to pick around the house and identify some items they hope to inherit! But I can say this firmly: Along with your stories, your family members are going to want some of your possessions. They just might not be the ones you'd expect.

THE CONVERSATIONS YOU DON'T LIKE HAVING

The best way to confirm who wants what is to ask. That might sound blindingly obvious, but it can sometimes be difficult to pose such direct questions. We don't want to address our own mortality, and our loved ones don't want to appear greedy. And I want to warn you up front that when you ask your loved one questions about your prized objects, you might not like the answers! I guarantee you that family and close friends *will* want some of your stuff—but they might not want what you expect them to want.

Finding out that others don't necessarily want your cherished belongings can be a painful experience. That prized tintype photo of your grandfather? Your son might just prefer to have it digitized. Your wedding dress? Your daughter might think that it's better suited to a thrift store than her closet. If there's something you own that your nephew previously told you he'd love to have—that sculpture or tie—he may have since changed his mind or discovered that he doesn't actually have the space for it.

Similarly, if your kids say they don't want something now, don't assume that once you're gone they'll have come to their senses and value it. I've had families tell me in reference to a daughter who rejected some item, "Well, she doesn't want it now, but she just doesn't know what she wants. She'll want it in a few years." Our adult kids are probably pretty clear on this—if they say no twice, it means no. You can sell it or give it to someone else who will appreciate it.

A partner or child isn't saying she doesn't love you when she rejects your suggested gifts. It's better to find out now rather than waiting until the moving truck shows up.

But if someone says no to your suggestions, ask what he *would* like of yours to help remember you. Your granddaughter may want your vintage 1960 Pucci dresses from the basement instead of your fancy china and crystal. Or perhaps your friend has always had his eyes on an old painting. Or she might want something you hadn't thought of altogether. Whatever the answer is, remember that it's not about what you want to give someone; it's about what he wants to keep your legacy alive. Often, the value to someone else of an object you own is emotional, not financial. Remember, the item is the vehicle to the story—the item isn't the story. Make sure your actions echo this insight. When you gift someone an item, explain why you want that person to have it. *That's* where the legacy lies. The *why* is what's important and may change someone's decision on wanting the item or not. I had one client who wanted to give her daughter a fragile snowflake Christmas tree ornament, but the ornament wasn't really her daughter's style. But if she had told her daughter why—because it had snowed on the morning she was born and she thought about her birth every time she hung the ornament—her daughter may have changed her mind. Sometimes the why is more important than the item. The story is the launch pad to a legacy.

If you're among a younger generation and reading this, I suggest that if you want something, say so. Don't be afraid to speak up. Tell your loved ones why their legacy matters to you, and what possession tells that story. I promise that if you do this, it will end up being one of the most important conversations of your life.

TIME LIMITS AND STIPULATIONS

Nicole was mindful of the permanence of her decisions: Once she selected any items, she wasn't going to be able to reverse her choices, because everything in the house would be sold or donated, and then the house would be sold. But often I see older generations gifting items temporarily. This process often goes wrong.

Frequently that's because the terms or time frame are unclear. If it's a loan, be super clear up front that it's a loan and that you do expect it back. A loan is not a gift, it's a loan. Also, if the item is on loan, take a picture of it with the camera on your phone and put a reminder in your calendar to ask for it back on the agreed-upon date.

Likewise, stipulations on a gift don't work. I've seen so many people give something with a condition attached to it. Saying things like, "You can have this hutch, which has been in our family for years, but I want you to put it in your living room." Don't do that! Once you give someone something, the item no longer belongs to you. Don't put the recipient in an awkward and beholden situation. I've seen this situation literally hundreds of times and it never ends up positive. (And yes, maybe your daughter-in-law did call me and ask me to put this specific tip in the book.)

IT'S OKAY TO SAY NO

Nicole had her choice of virtually everything in her grandparents' house. We were the only ones present. But, she generously suggested, "Maybe I should ask my parents what they want first." Since her parents had a full house of their own, and had encouraged Nicole to go through her grandparents' estate, she assumed they wouldn't want any of the items we saw in front of us. But to Nicole's surprise, her father named a number of items he wanted: an oil painting her grandparents had commissioned; his father's favorite pipe; and some of the board games the family had played together.

"Oh, I was thinking of taking the board games," Nicole told her father. Monopoly, backgammon, Risk—she, too, had memories of three generations laughing while they enjoyed those games together.

"Well, I'd rather have those for now, Nicole," her father said.

After they got off the phone, Nicole and I talked about her father's comments. She told me that she would defer to her father's wishes and relinquish any claim to the board games. She laughed because board games seemed such a childish thing to squabble over. But, I told her, she didn't care about the games themselves—she cared about the memories and stories that went with them. That was a very adult thing to be concerned about! I've seen families fight about items large and small. In the end, there is nothing small or silly about our feelings.

But Nicole was surprised that her father had wanted the games for himself rather than letting her have them. "That's not like him," she said. I want to be clear that she wasn't acting entitled to anything. Nicole was a person who oozed gratitude for her life and its blessings. She was just a bit taken aback at his strong feelings and wondered what was behind them. From our conversations, though, she understood that this was his Legacy List.

It was absolutely fine for him to refuse Nicole's request. Likewise, if *you're* not ready to part with your legacy items, that's okay, too. It's okay to say no when a loved one asks you for something that means a lot to you—just like it's okay when someone refuses your gifted item. My mother has a piano she inherited from her mother, which I played as a kid. My mom knows I've had my eyes on it for years, but she still plays it all the time and understandably wants to keep enjoying it. She has made it very clear to me that she will let me know when she is ready to pass it on to the next generation. That's her right to make that decision, and I'm proud that she is voicing her feelings.

NICOLE'S LEGACY LIST

In the days we worked together, Nicole and I discussed the value of legacy items, trying to identify her choices. She mentioned her grandparents' work ethic repeatedly, amazed and inspired by their ability to start a new life in a new continent and thrive through grit and ingenuity.

Nicole settled on a cardigan sweater her grandmother had worn, a symbol of her earthiness; a baking tray, which reminded Nicole of all the goodies they had baked; and some picture frames to replace her own. For every item she selected, Nicole told me its significance, encountering the memories the items aroused in her. The stories were remarkable, and I felt like I got to know people I'd never met in person. In recounting their lives to me, Nicole breathed more life into her family members. People live on forever if you tell their stories passionately to an interested audience.

Walking through the garage, we noticed on a shelf a coffee can filled with keys. Nicole stared at the can for a moment then pulled out one very rusty key.

"That was the key to Grandpa's truck," she said with a faint smile. "We used to drive everywhere in the truck." She had loved accompanying her grandfather as he went about his work in Richmond. With a chain of businesses that gradually sprawled across Virginia, he was often on the road, and Nicole would accompany him on the trips. She cherished those memories. They seemed to her to embody her grandparents' work ethic and admirable thriftiness.

"I could do something with those," Nicole said.

I didn't know what she meant—what are keys good for besides opening things?

She smiled at me. "Wind chimes," she said.

What?

Nicole took home the can of keys. Neil, with some craftsmanship, turned those keys into an incredible chime. Ever since, every time the wind blows, Nicole later told me, "It's like Grandpa is saying hello." When friends are over and comment on the unusual-looking chimes, Nicole tells them about her grandparents, the remarkable people who never stopped working so she could have a better life. The keys probably aren't the item her grandparents thought she'd want, but I know they'd be pleased with how their amazing story is told and retold. Sometimes if you tell the story enough, small items are the beginning of a lifelong legacy for generations to retell.

THE MAGIC OF UPCYCLING

Nicole's key wind chimes and my trolley tokens cuff links are examples of upcycling. The website Upcycle That uses this definition: "The act of taking something no longer in use and giving it a second life and new function. In doing so, the finished product often becomes more practical, valuable, and beautiful than what it previously was." Upcycling is a wonderful way of cultivating a legacy item. Among other advantages, you don't need to have anything financially valuable to upcycle something. In addition, the objects can be personal, idiosyncratic, and creative.

I've seen dozens of everyday, sometimes run-down, items transformed into legacy items through the magic of upcycling. Here are some of my favorites:

- **Jewelry.** Before my wedding, I had pieces of jewelry from my mom, both of my grandmothers, my grandfa-

Once Nicole chose her Legacy List items, the rest of our job became much easier. It was as though she felt freed to say goodbye to the pressure about what she should keep.

You can be in charge of your own legacy. That can sometimes be a revelation to people. You can be in charge of how you remember someone you love and *their* legacy. What are you

ther, my dad, and my great-uncle melted together to create my wedding band. I love that a ring I wear that symbolizes the love for my wife is a mixture of gold from all the people who loved and raised me and never met my amazing bride.

- **Buttons.** One of the most common items I find cleaning out homes is a metal Folgers coffee can filled with either pennies, nails, or buttons. I routinely encourage my clients to have everyone in their family pick one big ugly loud button and sew it to the bottom of their favorite jacket. Each time they're asked about the bizarre button, they get to tell the story of who it came from. Items are starting points to amazing stories.

- **Old clothes, from T-shirts to suits.** They make wonderful quilts or stuffed animals that make excellent legacy gifts for younger generations.

doing to make sure your legacy is being created? What do you want your great-grandkids, or anyone after them, whom you'll most likely never meet, to know about you? I don't mean that you have to stand out by setting a world record in the Olympics or write the next great American novel. I'm saying that you should think about telling your story to your loved ones. And that you should focus on that objective while decluttering and downsizing. Because the best way to guarantee a legacy is to create one.

That might sound difficult. It isn't. It just takes a little ingenuity and effort. The first thing to do is to find someone right away and tell them your favorite story about someone in your family. Write down the stories in a journal, or recount them aloud and record them, either audio or video. I have yet to meet a person who isn't curious about his ancestors, and your descendants will want to know about you and your family, too. Even some facts that might seem mundane to you—names, birth dates and places, occupations—will be of interest to generations that come after you. As you go about decluttering and downsizing, always remember how much this matters. *People don't miss stuff. They miss the people behind the stuff.*

A good Legacy List item is intensely personal, both to the giver and the receiver. You are now empowered to decide what constitutes a Legacy List item. Whatever your Legacy List items are, find a way to document them (write them down, take pictures or video, or record the stories) so the memory lives on forever, in case something ever happens to them. Start building a legacy now. It's essential to decluttering and downsizing—and moving on. But so is knowing what to donate and give away. I'll tell you about that in the next chapter.

STEP SIX

. . . .

Decide What to
Give Away

B&D Carpentry was legendary in central Maryland for being able to get any job done at a reasonable price. Ben and Darren, the team of brothers who co-owned the business for thirty years, had trained a younger generation of carpenters, painters, construction workers, and handymen who had spread across the state to practice their trades.

Ben retired first, but just before Darren was about to retire at age sixty-four, he passed away, leaving Ben to inherit the business and execute the estate of his best friend, brother, and business partner. So Ben called me and I took over much of the work of disbanding the company and closing out Darren's estate.

Ben was having trouble with three things that Darren had left him: tools, books, and magazines.

The tools were worth about $40,000, Ben told me. But to the dismay of Ben's wife and kids, who wanted the cash, he wanted to donate them—and he had someone in mind he wanted to give them to. No matter who you are, $40,000 is a lot of money. Ben was torn between heeding the wishes of his wife and children—none of whom were interested in carpentry or the business—and embracing the magic of giving, which he knew Darren would want him to do.

Darren's books and magazines posed a different problem. In addition to being a wonderful carpenter and father, he'd been a bibliophile, a master carpenter who had the knowledge base of a professor. His passion for reading was famous among his family and friends—he was the type of guy who would glance at a book in his lap while waiting at a stoplight, Ben told me. Ben didn't share his brother's passion for knowledge, but he thought that passing the books and magazines to other readers would be a better tribute to Darren than selling them for cash, if that were an option.

Ben's dilemmas were common—many people have difficulty knowing if, how, what, when, and where to donate their stuff. That's true for people giving their stuff to a family member, friend, or acquaintance they care about. And it's true for people considering gifting their things to a worthy charitable organization. Unless you've actually done it, donation seems so easy. Just throw it in a box and drop it off at a friend's home or the local donation center, right? Sometimes it's that easy, but often it's not. There can be all sorts of decisions involved in handing off items to someone you know, especially if you're facing external pressure to sell the items, like Ben, or have more than one person to choose from. Similarly, things can be complicated if you're opting for a nonprofit. How do you know which organizations are reputable? And what can and can't the organizations accept? More and more, charitable organizations are discerning about what they'll accept, unwilling to take items they know they can't use or give away. People often show me an item and ask me, "Should I sell this, or just give it away?" This chapter will walk you through all those situations.

Just as important, I encourage you to see the option of donating your stuff as a first resort, not a last one. In my career, I've seen that most people think they should donate the stuff they don't want. I want to change that mindset. Whether you're decluttering, downsizing, moving, or doing all three, strategically giving away many of your belongings can be both emotionally rewarding and a solution to your challenges. When you donate well, you maximize the impact your gift has on another person or cause. You're alive to the emotional gifts that you receive while donating. It isn't an afterthought or a practice you engage in reluctantly. In fact, I'm going to make the case for why you should donate items you probably haven't even thought of gifting—your good, intact belongings, not just your junk and throwaways. Giving away your things to neighbors, family members, friends, or people in your community or around the world can greatly enrich and enhance your life and the lives of others. And that, at the end of the day, is what we're after.

GIVE YOURSELF PERMISSION TO GIVE

Ben asked me outright what he should do with his brother's books, magazines, and tools. Oftentimes clients ask me to tell them what to do with their belongings. I never answer them. When people ask me that question, they already know what they want to do. What they're really asking for is not advice but reassurance that their choice is the right thing to do.

Consider Ben, who showed me his brother's massive tool collection in a huge warehouse at their old office building. It included a J.H. Williams 1,390-piece Mammoth tool set. There were also various power saws, tables, torques, and punching tools, plus lots of protective gear. Darren even had specialty tools that he had either made himself or picked up somewhere along the way. What should Ben do with them?

I thought I had an obvious answer. "What did his will instruct?" I asked.

Ben looked at me as if I had asked the most stupid question. Unfortunately, I'd gotten that reaction before. Darren's will, alas, hadn't specified what should be done with his tools, books, or magazines. Many people don't even write a will.

As executor of the estate, Ben was empowered to do whatever he wanted. Despite the pressure he was feeling from his family to sell, and the clear windfall he would receive, some powerful part of him was against the idea. I could see the decision in his face. I knew that voice inside him was critical.

Whenever there's an opportunity to make a buck, many of us feel compelled to take it. Sometimes, of course, we need the money. But often our culture tells us that we must pursue profit even when we don't need the money, or when the amounts we'd reap would be insignificant. I've seen families focus on selling an item even when they are only getting 5 percent of the value they paid for it. Even when their conscience was telling them something else. Even when they want to experience the unique rush that comes with gift-giving.

Grant yourself permission to experience that rush. To give away anything and everything you own. It's yours to do with as you wish—and if part of you feels the urge to donate your possessions, I encourage you to scratch that itch. For one thing, it'll make you happier than selling your stuff. Science backs me up on this. Research shows that giving makes us feel happy.

We're the only thing holding us back from luxuriating in that feeling. Yes, you are the only thing holding yourself back from feeling the joy of giving. But you can summon the courage to make different choices that are better for yourself and for others. Donating is one of those special choices that confers benefits to everyone involved in the situation.

At other times, you'll be reluctant to donate an item because you'll genuinely need or want to make some money on it. That's fine, too, of course. But don't confuse the emotional worth with the economic worth. You like something because you worked hard for it or it was given to you by a loved one who worked hard for it. But something is only worth financially what an independent third party will give you. And usually, for used items, that's not much. You need to allow yourself to accept that fact and move toward donating your stuff. I've never seen someone regret donating an item, because the emotional satisfaction giving generates always outweighs whatever loss is felt.

FIND YOUR MISSION

Ben and I talked about why he was thinking of giving away his brother's tools and print products. "They were all so special to Darren," he said. "It feels like they could be special to someone else, and that would be a great way to honor him." I agreed that it would. "I never met your brother," I said to him, "but I do know that improving the world through an act of generosity is always a great way to memorialize someone."

Ben nodded. "And I know exactly who'd love these tools," he said.

Both Ben and Darren had started as apprentices, and they knew how indispensable good mentorship had been to the development of their careers. That's why B&D Carpentry had an apprentice program, which had nurtured dozens of carpenters and handymen around the Maryland, Virginia, and Washington, D.C., region. Darren treated his apprentices like adopted sons, teaching them the age-old arts of woodworking, construction, and handiwork.

The last apprentice the company had hired was a young man named Kevin. He'd learned quickly and was eager to begin his career. But in addition to experience and know-how, there's one thing an up-and-coming carpenter needs to get steady work: good equipment. Kevin had a young family and couldn't afford all the tools he needed.

I could see Ben's face light up as he talked about how getting Darren's tools would be life-changing for Kevin. Ben's passion was evident, and by the end of our talk, he seemed to have forgotten all about the idea of selling off the equipment.

Ben had discovered his mission. Most people decide they want to give away some things and look for the most convenient place to drop them off. This is exactly backward. You want to identify your mission first. Your mission is the cause or individual you're most passionate about. It could be as close to you as your sibling or neighbor, as local as your community center down the street, or as international and broad as an animal rights or religious charity. Only you can decide which recipient is closest to your heart. Once you know your mission, you're likely to feel energized about donating.

There are thousands of charities wherever you live, but I look for "immediate use" charities that give items directly to help someone rather than putting them back on a retail shelf. Here are a few of my favorite charities that line up with my mission and passion. You'll see that I tend to give to organizations that help people who are poor or just need assistance, since I remember being without and can never forget the experience.

- Tech for Troops takes your electronics, such as outdated phones and televisions, and pays veterans to recycle them. It gives immediate jobs to people who can't find work while helping to repair the environment.
- Dress for Success accepts used women's work clothes in decent condition and gives them to people reentering the workforce, including single moms and ex-convicts.
- Soles4Souls takes gently used shoes and clothing and either gives them away or teaches people from underprivileged communities how to sell them.
- Local food banks serve people who simply don't have access to food. I was raised by one of the hardest-working single moms in the world, and the older I get, the more I realize how hard she worked to put food on our plates. Whether you are downsizing, decluttering, or moving, there is often a lot of food in your home that you can donate. Call to see what local food banks will and won't accept, and then take the extra few minutes and drop it off there. It will make an immediate difference. If you are moving, check out MoveForHunger.org to find a place to donate your food.

HOW TO RESEARCH CHARITIES

Sadly, a lot of scam artists operate in the world of charitable organizations. To avoid them, make sure that any organization you donate to is a registered nonprofit. The financial information of nonprofit organizations is public, and reputable groups usually have their important documents online or otherwise freely available. Perhaps most telling are a nonprofit's tax returns, which include reasonably detailed information about revenue and expenses as well as a list of officers, directors, and key employees who receive more than $100,000 in total compensation. To verify the credibility of a nonprofit, check out Charity Navigator, GuideStar, or the BBB Wise Giving Alliance, which evaluate and rate charities. (Find their contacts in the Resources.)

TAX ADVANTAGES

To take advantage of tax benefits, track your donations. All registered nonprofit organizations are required to issue receipts for donations over $250. For lesser amounts, they are required to give receipts upon request. Keep all this documentation with your tax records. You'll have to appraise the value of donated items, which you can do through online tools. Whether you can take a deduction for your donations, and how much you can deduct, depends on your tax situation, so you'll want to consult a professional.

DONATING BOOKS

I met Ben at Darren's home, a large apartment in a ten-story building, to assess the books and magazines. I've never seen so many books crammed into a space: 1,920 volumes to be exact, a mix of fiction, history, science, and philosophy.

"Darren inhaled books the way other people inhale air," Ben told me. "He loved surprising people who didn't expect a blue-collar worker to recite 'The Tyger' by William Blake by memory." Some shelves were double-stacked, with sets of books behind the ones you could see in the front. This guy loved

MAKE YOUR WISHES CLEAR

I've mentioned this in other chapters, and it's critical: Make your wishes known, through a will, letter of instructions, or another document. In my work, I see a lot of under-detailed wills like Darren's, and they can cause all sorts of problems and even heartache. The best way to ensure that your worldly possessions are gifted to the right people and causes after you're gone is to put it in writing. You won't just prevent confusion or disagreements about your stuff among your beneficiaries. You'll also force yourself to make difficult choices about what to pass on to whom.

Even if you're young, just starting out, or unsure who you want to leave your possessions to, document your wishes. In all my years in this industry, I've never heard anyone say they regretted making a will.

Online legal services exist that can help you create a will that handles the basics, but be sure it's flawless. A will

information. The magazines were on shelves in chronological order, like in a library. There were decades-old copies of *National Geographic*, *Life* (which isn't even published anymore!), and *Newsweek* (now only digital). I saw some yellowed newspapers, too.

Ben associated his brother so closely with a love of reading

is a complicated document with legal ramifications, and a poorly written will is worse than no will at all. Setting one up with a lawyer's help should, on the low end, cost around $300. It's not uncommon to pay much more if you have numerous beneficiaries, overseas assets, real estate, or a large number of possessions to dispense. Consider consulting an estate planning expert, who typically charges from $150 to $300 per hour. You don't need to own land or be wealthy to have an estate—the term just refers to anything a person owns. And be sure to discuss your plan with those who need to know.

I know this stuff is heavy, but I can't stress enough how important it is for you to get these things on paper so that you and your loved ones are protected. Part of decluttering and downsizing is getting your life in order. Many of my clients well into their forties, fifties, and sixties don't like talking about their estates. Please do, and talk to your family about it.

that he felt that selling all this paper would somehow dishonor Darren's memory. He said that in the back of his mind, he thought he himself should adopt the books, although he wasn't much of a reader.

Ben was less certain about what he wanted to do with his late brother's books than with the tools. Who would take all those? He called up a local used bookstore, which would buy only new hardcovers or bestselling paperbacks. Some of Darren's books were forty years old! Even the best of them were in only decent shape. Many were on esoteric topics, as you might expect from someone who "inhaled books."

I often tell clients that, whatever their situation, donating books is an excellent way to free up space. Books are bulky items. You don't need your own private bookstore in your home. In fact, unless you really need them as part of your profession, are a voracious reader, or just truly love books, you can get rid of almost all of them. We have been trained to see books as decorative items, but they're meant to be read.

I often find people holding on to their college textbooks years—even decades—after they graduated. Textbooks cost huge amounts of money and gave us our foundation of knowledge (assuming we read them—I've come across my share of unopened textbooks!), so people feel compelled to keep them. Well, I will argue that there is a slim chance you'll ever read those books again. You should have sold them the last week of that class and used the cash to buy your buddies a pitcher of beer. (I know I did.) Now you'll have to settle for giving them away.

When I was cleaning out my dad's house, I confess: I socked a lot of stuff into storage because I was sure that one day I'd use it.

That included a bunch of my dad's books, and I never read a single one though I had sworn I'd get around to it. After fifteen years, I got rid of all those books—after I'd spent thousands of dollars to keep them in storage. And as it turns out, I discovered the brilliance of libraries. Now, instead of buying all sixty-plus volumes of *Magic Treehouse* because I want my future grandkids (currently ages seven, nine, and eleven) to love the books as much as their fathers did, I'll visit the library when I actually need the book. It saves me space and money.

I suggested to Ben that we donate every single book to local libraries. He was so enthralled that you would have thought I'd invented the idea.

A lot of people are surprised to learn that many public libraries accept donations. Some accept used books only seasonally or during book drives, while others don't accept them at all. Check with your local institution to find out.

The library is a great place to donate books, because libraries will always be around and accessible to you, and your books would get a permanent home. Sometimes they hold book sales and use the money to buy current books. I've seen clients get excited about the concept of donating books to the library because they simply just wanted someone else to enjoy the books as much as they had.

Many of us have more books than we need. In one study, about one-quarter of Americans admitted to not having read a single book over the past year. It's okay if you're one of them! And even if you're more of a bookworm, libraries and bookstores and ebooks will be there for you in the future.

The Silver Spring public library was delighted when Ben called. It turned out the librarian actually knew Darren! In addition to buying books and magazines by the trunkful, he was a library devotee, too. The librarian told us that Darren had done some carpentry for the library branch and not told anyone—and he'd done it for free! I was amazed at this secret act of generosity and suddenly understood better why Ben was so insistent on memorializing his brother though donations. The library arranged a date for us to deliver all of Darren's books. Ben printed some stickers with his brother's name and the words "In Memory." We put those stickers in about a hundred books before we loaded them on the truck, so that future readers who opened the pages would acknowledge the generous man who made their reading adventure possible. Ben has since visited the library to admire the volumes bearing his brother's name on the shelves for patrons to enjoy. It's an excellent legacy.

If your public library doesn't accept some or all of your book donation, here are some other places where you can pass on the wonders of learning:

- **School libraries.** Reader to Reader, Inc. is a wonderful non-profit that has provided more than $50 million worth of books and computer equipment to school and public libraries in some of the poorest parts of the country. It accepts books in good condition suitable for teens and children, with the exception of textbooks and encyclopedias.

- **Little Free Libraries,** where neighbors can leave and take books. If you don't see one in your town or city, you can build one!

- **Book drives.** Schools and community organizations frequently hold book drives to raise money and collect books for people in need.

- **Thrift stores.** Most donation centers and independent thrift shops have a shelf for books.

- **Nonprofit organizations.** Some charitable groups accept books, including Goodwill, Habitat for Humanity ReStores, the Salvation Army, and Vietnam Veterans of America.

- **Local museums, historical societies, higher education institutions, and performing arts groups.** Ask these groups if they want certain types of books.

- **Prison libraries and literacy programs.** Most states have programs that distribute books to inmates. Books Through Bars, for example, sends books to inmates in Pennsylvania, New York, New Jersey, Delaware, Maryland, and Virginia.

The Prison Book Program operates in Massachusetts. To find a program near you, search for "books to prisoners."

- **Armed forces charities.** Operation Paperback, for example, is a charity serving individuals in the military and personnel deployed overseas or housed in hospitals or rehabilitation facilities.

One final note on books: If you can't find a place to take your books, local book recyclers, which you can find online, might give you about two and a half cents per pound for them. But it's a lot better than paying someone like me a hundred bucks an hour to come and take them all away.

TREASURE HUNT

When sorting through books, make sure you look through every page, because we often find cash and important letters inside.

DONATING CLOTHES

If you're trying to declutter and are facing the problem of culling through your clothes, it's easy to tell yourself that you'll wear any item at some point down the road. So my rule is this: Unless you're going to wear it in the next six months, get rid of it (sell, donate, or trash). The only exception is seasonal clothes. You get a free pass on those, but be honest with yourself and get rid of the clothes you really don't wear anymore.

If you are having trouble thinning out your wardrobe, hold a small fashion show. Usually, two things happen: First, just trying on things will convince you to toss a lot of the clothes. We all age and outgrow styles and sizes. I used to save my size 28, then 30, then 32 jeans because I kept telling myself that I would slim down someday. But the reality is, I'm a snug size 36. I'll keep the 34s as an inspiration to cut back on the ice cream, but I've accepted that the slimmer sizes are unrealistic. I don't have space in my closet for them anymore because I don't have space in my fantasy life for them.

Second, a fashion show forces you to show off the clothes to other people in your family. If people laugh at your bell-bottom jeans, it's probably time to let them go. If an article of clothing you are partial to is out of style, a brutally honest twelve-year-old will let you know. At the fashion show stage, I suggest letting the family vote.

When it's time to get rid of the clothes, you can ask friends or relatives who wear that size if they'd like them. Selling some of these clothes to a vintage shop will make you a little money, and we'll discuss those options in Step Seven. The rest can go to donations, which we'll discuss below. For now, be honest with yourself about what fits your body and your lifestyle, and get rid of the clothes you don't currently wear.

If someone is deceased, the first and easiest decision is to get rid of most of his or her clothes. They're probably not your style or size. But clothes are not just random pieces of threads. Sometimes they are meaningful, individualized garments that can define a person. Sometimes certain rare items can be passed down from generation to generation, so that your grandfather's jacket becomes one you wear every day. I generally recommend keeping one or two outfits that make you smile. Many of my clients who have lost a spouse put off cleaning out their deceased partner's clothes. It's understandable: There are smells and feelings attached to all of those clothes. Clients will ask me, "When will I know it's time to let go?" All I can tell you is, if you are asking that question, it's not time yet. You'll know when it's time. One day you'll just decide today is the day and you'll do it.

As I went through my dad's stuff, I'd picture him in every article of clothing that was hanging in the closet or buried in a drawer. When I saw a pair of silly pants, I'd remember the one time he wore them. Or my favorite: a ridiculous tweed jacket— silver with green fluorescent streaks that looked like something a drunk painter designed—that he wore one evening trying to pick up a woman (a futile attempt, I'm sure).

The reality is, unfortunately, that clothes are especially difficult to sort through—they are very personal, specific to an individual. That's true with Michael Jackson's glove, it's true with Marlon Brando's leather jacket, and it's true with people in *your* life. Oftentimes the clothes will even *smell* like the person who has worn them. Still grieving, I would put my nose in Dad's clothes just to remember what it was like to have him around.

In the end, though, I was able to get rid of most everything. I kept only two of his awesomely absurd Tom Selleck–like, *Magnum P.I.*–ish Hawaiian shirts—which, to my son's dismay, I still proudly wear.

TELL THE STORIES OF THE STORIES

There's a catch to my advice about donating anything, and by now you know what I'm going to say: You need to tell the stories about the items you're donating. It was genuinely a joy to hear about Darren's love of books. It reminded me of my father's. He, too, loved reading. In the last weeks before he died, I would pull one of the many books from his shelf and ask him to tell me about it. All I had to do was show him the book and its title, and he would regale me with the book's plot, characters, and value—and then he would tell me about *his* life at the time he'd read the book. He relayed the challenges and joys of his life then, and why the book was an amazing escape or enhancement to experience. When you tell the story of a book, you get the author's intended story, but you also get a snapshot of the reader's life when the book was read. Tell the story surrounding a book, and it's much easier to get rid of it. Then another person can enjoy the book as much as you did.

THE PROBLEM OF PERIODICALS

Darren's books were taken care of, but his magazines and newspapers were another matter. Ben found that libraries and charities had no interest in them. I had warned him that was likely to happen. All major and most minor magazines and newspapers dating back centuries are archived in databases like LexisNexis and Factiva, accessible at any university library and many big-city public libraries. Still, my clients are often reluctant to toss out old *National Geographic* and *Life* magazines. Sometimes they've saved newspapers marking historic occasions, like Neil Armstrong's steps on the moon or John F. Kennedy's assassination. But digitization has made print copies of newspapers and magazines unnecessary, if not obsolete. Some items you're having trouble parting with might be one of a kind or irreplaceable—

but magazines and newspapers aren't among them. If you doubt me, just search for your most prized newspaper or magazine on the internet. There are almost certainly copies to read or buy there. So put yours up for auction! And if they don't receive bids, dear reader, you can discard them in good conscience knowing that their existence is safe and secure in libraries across the country. There's no need to hold on to them, because someone else has done that for you.

ONLINE FREECYCLING

But there may be someone who wants your old magazines. Before you toss them, you have options.

Ben decided to post an ad on Craigslist offering his brother's magazines to an appreciative reader. Craigslist's free classified ads reach a wide local audience. It's used for both donating and selling stuff, which I talk about in Step Seven. In my experience, you can connect directly with people in need who tell you they can make use of your items. That's deeply gratifying. Often recipients will offer to meet wherever you prefer to pick up whatever you're donating. And I haven't come across many scam artists on Craigslist when donating, because no money is being exchanged.

Several people responded to Ben's ad. Some wanted additional details about the publications, while others expressed interest but then seemed to disappear. That's typical. Finally, after several days, a woman named Sally responded. She was a history buff who jumped at the possibility of scouring through old newspapers and magazines. Sally told Ben that she hadn't been trolling Craigslist for anything in particular—she just had limited economic means and astutely sought out things other people were selling at a discount or giving away. This was exactly the type of person he hoped to reach. Ben and I lugged boxes filled with Darren's periodicals out of his apartment building and down on the street. At an agreed-upon time, Sally showed up in her car and we piled the boxes into her trunk. She seemed so glad to get Darren's magazines and newspapers, and Ben was happy to see them getting a new life in a new home.

There are many outlets online for your donations besides Craigslist, of course. Here are some of the most popular. As with anything online, beware of scammers and take precautions to protect your privacy.

- **"Buy Nothing" groups on Facebook.** Many cities, large towns, and rural areas have local Buy Nothing groups, where users give away items they no longer use. With nearly three billion monthly users, Facebook has unparalleled reach. One advantage of these groups is that you can opt to donate your goods there after trying to sell them on Facebook Marketplace. I use this for almost all my donations now. By the time this book comes out, Buy Nothing should also offer an app.

- **Nextdoor.** This is a well-known neighborhood-based social networking site and app. People must be verified in specific neighborhoods. You can post what you want to give away, or use its "Sell for Good" feature, which allows users to sell items and direct the proceeds to local nonprofits, including animal shelters, parent/teacher associations, and after-school programs.

- **Freecycle.** This is one of my favorite websites, since its express purpose is for people to distribute their goods to others. Also, unlike Facebook and Nextdoor, it's a nonprofit organization.

MATT'S FIVE RULES FOR GIVING ITEMS AWAY ONLINE

1. Describe the items concisely and completely. Answer as many questions as possible in advance, so that you don't

WHERE TO DONATE SPECIFIC STUFF

- **Bibles.** I've found as many as six generations of family Bibles collecting dust in storage. How did they get there? Probably each generation felt guilty about throwing them out! Don't be victimized by tradition. Ask family members if they would like to have them. If you get no takers, donate the Good Books to an area church.
- **National flags.** People who own national flags tend to believe strongly in their national identity. For them, the flag is a potent symbol. Honor those beliefs by disposing of the flag in a respectful way. Check with a local veterans' group or Boy Scout or Girl Scout troop. They may offer a ceremony to dispose of your flag properly, if needed, and as a bonus the scouts can receive a badge for helping you with your flags (for real).
- **Military uniforms.** If you have an old military uniform, you'll want to keep the patches, hat, and any medals. These can be stored in a cigar box and passed down to an interested family member or made into a great keepsake. To learn where to donate the uniform, call the local office of the corresponding armed services branch and ask about organizations that accept donations. Remember, it's the act of service you are commemorating, not the piece of cloth itself.
- **Wedding dresses.** When cleaning out the attic of a recent

client, we found three generations of wedding dresses. Seeing them lined up was lovely, but in all their years of storage, how many times do you think they saw the light of day? Probably none, since they were passed on by their prior owners. If you can't bear to let go of your own wedding dress, keep it. But if you're holding on to Great-Grandma's because you think you should, don't. Ask family members if it's something they would like to have. Younger generations may want to have the dress altered. If the answer is no, donate the dress to a charity that accepts clothing or costumes.

- **Trophies.** I've found a few Olympic Silver medals, which families opted to sell or keep, but most trophies—though hard-earned—are, frankly, worthless. For local sports, my advice is to contact the team to see if it wants it. But if we're talking a chipped gold-painted metal cup stamped with "1986 Bowling Champion," give yourself permission to toss it in the trash.

- **Sports uniforms.** What about Dad's old varsity letter jacket? If he was famous, finding a buyer will be easy. Otherwise, a younger family member might want the jacket. If that doesn't work, again, donate or sell it to a used or vintage clothing shop. Believe it or not, someone would love to transform it into a trendy vintage piece. The risk is thinking that *we* will turn it into a trendy piece. The reality is, if we haven't already, we won't in the future. Be honest with yourself on your skill set and time available for new projects.

have to spend a lot of time responding to emails asking questions about item details. Ben wisely listed the dates and issues of the newspapers and magazines he was giving away. Have a tape measure on hand and write down the dimensions. I assure you the recipient will want to know the sizes, no matter what the item.

2. Post a current photo of the item you're selling. Ben snapped pictures of the covers of the magazines and the front pages of the newspapers he was offering. Those visuals made all the difference in making the items more enticing. Prospective recipients could see that the publications were in good condition and that they were real; keep in mind that recipients have to be on the lookout for scams, too.

3. Offer only one means of contact. I recommend email. Personally, I never post my phone number, because people can call and text your phone, and spammers love to use phone numbers. Never post your address. And when calling someone, I use the *67 feature before my number to block the recipient from seeing it.

4. If at all possible, arrange to have the buyer pick up the item somewhere other than your home. If that's not possible, have someone at home with you.

5. Ignore inquiries that ask about shipping the item or request your financial information for a bank transfer. These are not legitimate.

THE POWER OF GIVING

We piled all of Darren's old tools into my moving truck and drove them over to Kevin's house one afternoon when his wife said he'd be at home. Kevin was surprised when we pulled into his driveway, and even more surprised when we called him over and opened the back.

"Darren would want you to have these," Ben told him.

I'll never forget the look on Kevin's face. He knew that this gift was life-changing—and he knew that Ben knew that, too. Both men began crying at the magnificence of the occasion—a once-in-a-lifetime experience for us all. Kevin would be able to open his own carpentry business, to carry on the tradition he'd learned from the man whose tools he was inheriting. And he'd be able to have apprentices of his own and would one day tell them of the brothers whose generosity made their working lives possible. It was incredible to watch a true living legacy in action. I couldn't imagine a better tribute to Darren, and I knew that Ben was glad he listened to his heart and gave the gift of a lifetime.

The reality is that, in all likelihood, most of your items aren't life-changing or worth tens of thousands of dollars. But you can experience the same good feelings that Ben did when you give the right things to the right people or organization at the right time. You'll also feel good letting go of those items and moving on. That said, there are still probably some big-ticket items you're hoping to make some cash on. I'll talk about how to do that in the next chapter.

. . . .

Decide What to Sell (and Where to Sell It)

MARY RAN A BELOVED LOCAL restaurant and bar that was a gathering place in her small hometown, tucked in the foothills of the Blue Ridge Mountains in Appalachia. She was boisterous and fun-loving, her laugh the soundtrack of her restaurant.

If she wasn't at work, Mary, whose husband had died a few years earlier, was visiting one of her four daughters—two who lived nearby, one in California, and another in New York—and her grandkids. Mary wasn't cherished just by her family; she was adored by her customers and the community at large.

She lived in a large white Victorian with black shutters and a sizable yard. It had a roomy screened porch with lush greenery on every side. The problem was, she was rarely there. She kept herself so busy with work and family that the house frequently sat empty. Such a large place—one that had once suited her family of six—just didn't make sense for this single, on-the-go grandmother. So she found a much smaller house in town, closer to work and to two of her daughters, and much more manageable.

Mary had a lifetime's worth of possessions that she had already sorted through. Before I came into the picture, she had already identified what she absolutely had to keep, what she would donate, what she wanted to give to family, and what she needed to sell. Her next step was actually selling the stuff, which she needed help to do as efficiently, painlessly, and quickly as possible. That's where I came in. She had seen me on television and liked my Southern twang. I drove out to work with her for several weeks.

Her for-sale list included clothes, jewelry, her late husband's record collection, and furniture. And at the top of the list was an antique grandfather clock. It was an incredible timepiece, passed down from her grandmother, with hand-carved details, lovely aged wood, and a mechanism that still kept perfect time. She told me that growing up she had always loved the sound of that clock chiming the hour. It was the pulse of Mary's large house for decades. Ideally, she would have passed the clock on to her daughters—they all had fond memories of it, too. But none of them wanted it. They had their own small houses, growing families, and abundant possessions. She really wanted to keep the heirloom in the family, but the reality was that no one, including Mary, had space for this amazing clock in their life now. I gradually got her comfortable with the reality of letting it go, and we prepared to sell it along with the other items.

So here she had her for-sale list, but she didn't know where to start: What was the financial value? What would the items actually sell for? Where are the best ways or places to sell them? By then, I'd had a decade of experience selling just these kinds of items. Once my clients have sorted to this point and are clear about what they're ready to part with, the next step is fairly easy. We walk through the pile to see what might bring in some cash.

Here's what none of my clients want to hear: You won't get rich. But you will be able to get rid of clutter so you can move forward in your life. That, after all, is what really matters. People tend to focus on how much money they want to make instead of the life they want to live. But spending countless hours torturing yourself because your beloved items aren't worth what you'd hoped is not a path to peace of mind or to moving forward. Selling, like all stages of decluttering, can be an intense, emotional process. The best thing you can do is remember your goal instead of getting caught up in the nitty-gritty. By keeping your ultimate objectives top of mind, you can get done with the business of selling and get on with the business of living.

Let's walk through this step by step.

SET LOW EXPECTATIONS

When I met Mary, she'd already done a lot of emotional work and most of the heavy lifting of sorting, donating, and discarding. She was looking forward to finally doing something exciting. She said, "It's time to sell stuff and make some money!"

"*Some* money," I said. She looked at me with raised eyebrows.

"Remember, our goal is to help you get rid of possessions in your home, not get rich," I said. She nodded. I knew that she might not like hearing that. But it's my job to tell the truth to people I'm working with, even when it's unpleasant. Sadly, selling off our stuff is not just a matter of posting an ad and collecting fistfuls of dollars. The ruthless process of assessing your stuff comes first. I've found that people usually overestimate the financial value of their objects.

For one thing, we all work long and hard for what we own. My clients don't look around their homes and ask themselves how much their objects are worth compared to countless other identical objects in the marketplace. They see the sweat and sacrifice that went into buying all those belongings. What's more, we confuse the sentimental value of our objects with the financial value they'll have to others. It's only human to believe our stuff is worth more than it actually is because we attach emotions and memories to those items. That beautiful beaded necklace one client bought when working with the Peace Corps in Africa—having a delightful conversation with the artist, agonizing over which color to buy—is invaluable to her. But honestly, it's probably worthless on the open market thirty years later. Selling our belongings means separating the powerful emotional value from the brutal financial reality of what these possessions are worth in the marketplace.

In addition, it's just a fact that most of the items we buy in our consumer culture lose value over time. My clients think their possessions are worth more than they actually are because they paid hard-earned cash for them. A Steinway piano, maybe. But that dining room hutch you love so much? It might have cost you, back in the day, the equivalent of a month's salary. It might have been your pride and joy during those fun and memorable holiday family dinners. All that money you paid gets mixed up with all the cherished memories. That makes the hutch seem even more valuable. Unfortunately, people aren't interested in compensating you for whatever you originally paid, or even what a new hutch is worth today—they're only willing to pay you what your used hutch is worth now relative to comparable items out there.

I work hard to temper my clients' expectations and remind them of our goal: a less cluttered life. As strange as it sounds, the money is not the important thing. The right mindset for this stage is to focus on getting everything sold, no matter how much money it brings in. The goal in selling our possessions is not to make a windfall profit (although that is a nice bonus when it happens!); it's to move the process forward as efficiently, painlessly, and smoothly as possible.

You have already decided that these items weren't important enough to keep. That decision has been made. "Think of your clock as already gone," I told Mary. "It's not even yours anymore. Any money you now get for it is gravy." Repeat after me: A possession is only worth what someone will pay for it, not what you may think it's worth. Usually, the latter is higher than the former. Sometimes way higher. That's the awful truth.

DETERMINING REAL VALUE

Given my previous experience selling grandfather clocks, I estimated Mary's was worth a few thousand dollars. "That sounds like a good chunk of change," she said. But, I warned her, just because an item is worth something doesn't mean it will command that amount on the market at any given time. If, for some random reason, a bunch of grandfather clocks hit the regional market right then, she wouldn't be able to get what she might have a year earlier. Mary was becoming realistic—I think she appreciated my honesty.

If you don't have a professional on hand, you'll have to form an idea of what value the market puts on similar items. Start by looking online. Check eBay, Craigslist, Amazon, or any sites that sell items likes yours. For valuable items, I've also used WorthPoint, a fee-based website that accumulates sales information on thousands of items from estates sales around the world. This won't guarantee your final selling price, of course, but if you check out similar items being sold on several websites, you'll get a good sense of what you'll get from a sale (minus any fees you have to pay, which I'll go into later). That up-front work will save you the effort down the road of repeatedly taking your items off the market, lowering the price, and then putting them back on the market.

Larger or rarer items may be worth a considerable amount. If you suspect that's the case, you may want to have the value professionally appraised. Appraisers will use their detailed understanding of niche marketplaces to provide you with expert guidance in pricing. An appraiser can help you avoid pricing items too low—or too high. If I didn't have experience with grandfather clocks over the years, I would have suggested that Mary meet with an appraiser.

Reputable appraisers are certified and accredited through one or both of two organizations: the International Society of Appraisers (ISA) or the American Society of Appraisers (ASA). Each has several levels of certification relating to years of experience, specialization, and other factors. The greater the appraiser's certification, the more advanced the expertise, and the higher the appraisal fee. Regardless, appraisers accredited from these organizations are bound by a code of ethics. For instance, legitimate appraisers will not ask for a percentage of the sale or offer to buy the item being appraised—instead, you'll be charged an hourly fee, flat rate, or per item charge. Be ready to spend $300 to $500 on average for a standard appraisal, although the cost can be higher. Obviously that's a hefty fee, so you have to determine how much an item might reasonably fetch in the marketplace to determine if getting an appraisal makes sense.

Keep in mind as you're doing preliminary price research that monetary value is determined by a combination of quality and rarity. Old does not equal rare. That 1967 set of *Encyclopaedia Britannica* your parents scrimped and saved for? It's not worth its weight in paper now. Thousands upon thousands of those sets were published, so they aren't rare. Although the physical books and information inside them are of high quality, all that information is now available for free online, where it is also updated regularly. Those sets hold virtually no value. There are, unfortunately, a lot of possessions like that. I don't know how many full sets of *Sports Illustrated* and *National Geographic* back issues I've pulled out of attics, but I do know the homeowners in each case thought that they were saving something financially valuable. They were wrong.

For Mary's jewelry, I called in a friend of mine, Vijay, who is accredited by the International Society of Appraisers. He charged us $500 to come to Mary's home and sort through her rings, necklaces, and bracelets.

"I estimate the whole collection is in the $10,000 to $12,000 range," he said. He sat with us and item by item provided his recommendations on what we should ask from buyers. I don't think Vijay gave Mary the numbers she wanted to hear. Appraisers rarely do. People watch shows like *Storage Wars* and *Antiques Roadshow* and buy into the fantasies. But I can firmly say that suddenly discovering an item in your attic or basement that commands hundreds of thousands of dollars is extremely rare. A depressing rule of thumb is that your items are almost certainly worth less than what you hope. Fortunately, Mary knew that her clothes and vinyl collection weren't worth paying Vijay to assess.

Once she had a realistic sense of what her possessions were worth, it was time to decide where to sell them.

WHERE TO SELL

As you read through the options below, think back to what I said about being realistic when it comes to financial value versus emotional value. The ultimate point is that you have to keep telling yourself that the decision has already been made to part with the item. The options are numerous, so I'll go through the most important ones that I use in this section:

- Facebook Marketplace and eBay (there are countless other online sites, but I find these get the most eyeballs)

- Estate sales and their cousins, yard and garage sales
- Consignment shops
- Local classified ads
- Pawnshops
- Auction houses

THE SPREADSHEET SOLUTION

I always tell my clients, "Let it be a spreadsheet issue. Let the math make the decision." I usually have to say that quite a few times before it sinks in, because the emotional pull of the stories is so darn strong. But using spreadsheets to price our items is the easiest way to make more objective decisions. Find a bunch of related items for sale online and in local classifieds and put them, line by line, in the spreadsheet, along with the prices. If all the used grandfather clocks you can find are offered at prices around $500, deciding to sell yours for $1,000 is bad math. Saying to yourself, "But I paid *X* for this" is just a mental stumbling block in the process. *Profit* or *perceived value*—take those terms out of your vocabulary for now. They cannot be a consideration if you're going to make it through this stage of the process with limited pain and stress. Let the spreadsheet handle it.

MATT'S EIGHT RULES FOR SELLING ONLINE

1. The more complete the listing, the better. It's wise to be totally honest about the condition of the item, including the flaws. Include measurements, too. This is your chance to head off a cascade of questions from interested parties who want to know more than what you put in the listing.
2. List the shipping options and cost.
3. Post as many pictures as you can. Sharp, high-quality photos are a sign of a serious, honest seller and help draw eyeballs to your listing. But make sure there is no personal information in the background of the picture. Posting a picture of a bicycle with your house numbers in view can be dangerous.
4. Be responsive. If you're going to make the most of online selling, you have to play the game and respond to any messages as quickly, courteously, and completely as possible. It's true that selling online can try your patience. The messages you get from buyers will test that old adage "There are no stupid questions." Someone

Facebook Marketplace

For all items that will sell for less than about $5,000, Facebook Marketplace is now my go-to. I've found it's an easy and safe

once asked me if I would accept $1,000 in Japanese coins for a leather chair I was selling. But if you don't respond quickly and positively, the potential buyer will be wary that you're not a reputable seller and go looking for a similar listing on which to spend his or her money.

5. Set the price a little higher than what you want to receive, but not too much higher or no one will look at your ad. I generally assume I will be selling at about 25 percent less than the price I've set.

6. If the item doesn't sell in twenty-four hours, your price is probably too high. Drop the price immediately by 10 to 25 percent.

7. Don't let your pride get in the way when negotiating. It's a two-way dance, and remember that you already decided you don't want the item. Don't ruin a sale over a $5 difference. Turning down a buyer over $5 or $10 may cost you an hour or more of your time, and your time is worth something. If you have a person who wants to buy your stuff, find a way to get it done.

8. If you don't sell in five days, set your lowest price. If it's not gone in a day, you're done. Donate the item. The reality is that, at this time, there's no market for your item. Don't take it personally.

place to sell stuff. Most people you know use the site, as do most of the people they know. Marketplace is organized locally, so you can search prospective buyers' profiles to determine their trustworthiness. You can receive payment electronically and even organize pickup without coming face-to-face with the buyer, if you prefer. Furniture, which is normally difficult to sell online when you're not local because delivery costs are high and it's difficult to assess quality, usually sells on Facebook Marketplace, with its massive local audience. You'll have to lower your expectations on price, but you won't have to hire someone like me to take it away.

eBay

eBay is an auction website that best serves commercial sellers who buy and sell as part of an ongoing business. Compared to Facebook Marketplace, I have found it more difficult to use and less effective for declutterers who may only need it once. And with 185 million users, it lacks Facebook's three-billion-strong global reach. I haven't used eBay myself in a very long time. That said, if you or someone you know is comfortable with the technology, go for it.

Estate Sales

Mary didn't want to have an estate sale, which I was glad about. I'm not a fan of estate sales, based on both personal and professional experience. I was responsible for downsizing my grandparents' mountain home in Colorado in 2002 and opted for an estate sale. The number of potential buyers was severely limited by the inaccessibility of the property. Not even a hundred people showed up for the whole day, and we sold far fewer possessions than I had hoped to. I felt like a kid who invites everyone from class to his birthday party and no one shows up.

In hindsight, my grandfather's vintage farming equipment and my grandmother's jewelry could have actually brought in good prices if I had put them up for auction. The problem of a limited audience is a common one to estate sales that are not also online. You're dealing with local shoppers in an estate sale—just as with garage or yard sales—who don't show up hoping to spend a premium on your cherished possessions. In fact, I sometimes tell my clients, "You're just having a yard sale indoors." Shoppers are coming to get the best bargain possible, just as they would at a yard or garage sale. No one goes to a yard sale with the intention of overpaying for something. Estate sales also attract plenty of browsers, window-shoppers who are just looking at your stuff and wandering through a house.

There is, though, one big benefit I see to an estate sale, and here's how you can exploit it. If the house is being sold as part of your downsizing process, the estate sale can be used as an easy way to draw people in and show the house. Alert the real estate agent and have fliers on hand for potential buyers.

Yard and Garage Sales

Mary asked if we should consider a yard sale. I've done my share of them over the years, especially in my work with hoarders. It's easy to just set one up as a staging location for everything we pull out of the house. I don't see the same value for my downsizing and decluttering clients, though. I've found that when they suggest a yard sale, they inevitably have unrealistic expectations of how much money they will make. I feel that the entire goal of a yard sale buyer is to get the best bargain; your goal is the opposite. That's just a recipe for a bad outcome.

A yard or garage sale should be a last resort. If the point is to get rid of all your stuff, you should know that there is a good chance you'll be sitting in your lawn chair surrounded by a lot of leftover possessions at the end of the day. A yard sale also sucks up much more time and effort than most people realize. It might look easy, but in terms of pure time spent, it usually takes about fifty hours to set up and execute. Estimating that your time is worth $20 an hour, that's $1,000 worth of your time! You'll have to work pretty hard to make it successful, and you have to be stone-cold ready to deal with some odd characters.

But if downsizing or decluttering leaves you with a huge number of smaller items that retain a reasonable amount of perceived value ("perceived" by the person on the street, not you), a yard sale may be a decent option. The trick is to make transactions as easy as possible for both buyers and yourself. The only good thing about a yard sale is that sometimes someone comes by at the end and makes an offer on everything. An extremely low-priced offer, no doubt, but it's a great way to remove everything you do not want.

FOOLPROOF TIPS FOR SUCCESSFUL ESTATE AND YARD SALES

If you decide to have an estate or yard sale, follow these guidelines:

- **Set a date and strict hours for the sale.** Stick to those. Beware: People will try to come early to grab extraordinary bargains. If that isn't okay, say so in your promotions. But be prepared: If you post that it starts at 9 a.m., be outside at 7 a.m. because people will show up early.
- **For yard sales, come up with a Plan B for bad weather.**
- **Compose and maintain an inventory.** You can write it up by hand or use a computer program like Excel. I've also used

a software program called FairSplit (FairSplit.com), which lets multiple family members track estate assets. The point is to list everything you want to sell. This can be a big benefit for people helping you with the sale—it means they won't be asking you questions every five minutes. An inventory can also be a way to track what's sold and for how much. If you're holding the sale following the death of a friend or relative, the inventory may be key to listing assets in probate or for other tax issues involving the estate.

- **Photograph all the items before you start the sale.** That way you can look back at any time to see what you did or didn't sell. As you probably know by now, downsizing and decluttering can be super exhausting, and it's common to soon forget what you sold. The pictures also may come in handy later if you are settling an estate or need them for legal reasons.

- **Organize and group items.** I always group items in a display by price—say, a table where everything costs $5. Trust me, this makes your life a whole lot easier than if you have to write up price tags for every single item you're selling.

- **Offer deals on combined sales.** The point is to get rid of this stuff. If someone is haggling about the price of a baseball mitt and bat, offer to give them a discount if they'll take the soccer balls and goal net, too.

- **Enlist help.** Theft and home damage are usually not big issues during estate sales, but they can occur. You'll head off any problems by having several relatives or friends spend the day as your eyes and ears in different parts of the house while also taking money and answering questions about any items on sale (or sending prospective buyers your way).

- **Block off private areas and whatever isn't for sale.** This is common sense but something many individuals fail to do before an estate sale. Be as blatant as possible in marking off no-go zones. Spend a couple bucks and buy a roll of yellow caution tape to hang across stairs or doorways.

- **Keep it neat and clean.** Don't overcrowd displays, and keep pathways clear for smooth traffic flow. If you're going to the trouble of hosting an estate sale, you should make it as easy as possible for shoppers to move around and see everything.

- **Advertise.** Success is a numbers game. You need to draw in as many people as possible because only a small percentage are going to translate to actual sales. Advertise on Facebook; Craigslist; local sites such as Nextdoor; and in the local newspaper; and post fliers at local community centers, supermarkets, or on any other community bulletin boards. Add color pictures to entice potential buyers for bigger or high-dollar items. And yes, I said local newspaper ads. They're relatively inexpensive, and people still look at them for estate and yard sales.

Consignment

Consignment was the avenue we chose for Mary's clothing.

Selling items through a consignment shop may seem like an ideal alternative for the declutterer or downsizer, but it rarely is for most items. I used to suggest that clients sell nice furniture at a consignment shop, for instance, but those days have passed. The problem is that most consignment shops don't have enough foot traffic or an online presence to get your stuff the amount of exposure that would lead to a decent sales price. The shop owner usually has to move the item as quickly as possible to make whatever money she can and free up room in the store. Over my twenty-plus years in the business, consignment sales have consistently declined. What you'll earn for your hassle (delivering the item and checking in regularly to see if it sold) is rarely worth what you'll make on the sale.

The one exception seems to be clothing. You can make a good amount of money quickly by emptying an overstuffed closet and consigning all the clothes you'll never wear again, or with those boxes and boxes of baby outfits in the attic that were worn only a couple of times. Vintage clothing does especially well on consignment. Mary earned a good amount of money selling her daughters' old clothes on consignment. Some shops will buy the clothes directly from you at a low price, while others will take 50 to 60 percent of the sale for themselves. The shop we worked with got 60 percent of each sale, leaving Mary with just 40 percent, but even so, with boxes full of clothes, the actual dollar amount was significant. On the other hand, years ago I was helping an elderly couple downsize their home, and the wife insisted on consigning her impressive, fifty-year-old collection of bone china. Those plates held a lot of emotional value for her but weren't worth much to the shop owner, and apparently even less to the consignment shop's clients. After three weeks, the shop owner called to tell the woman she needed to pick up the china because it wasn't selling and he wanted to free up room in the shop for other items. That client actually lost money, because she had to hire someone to deliver—and then pick up—the china.

Local Classifieds

Classified ads in local newspapers and other publications can seem an obvious way to sell possessions directly and quickly. My issue with classifieds is that while they can seem pretty inexpensive, you have to wonder what you're getting for that

FOUR STEPS TO FINDING THE RIGHT CONSIGNMENT SHOP

1. **Check out the store.** Pretend you're a shopper. How organized and appealing is the stock? If things are crammed in, your stuff is unlikely to get the attention it needs to sell. Is the shop in a busy location? Does there seem to be a reasonable amount of foot traffic? This is your chance to scout for success and weed out any shop that is off the beaten path.

2. **The closer, the better.** A shop that is nearby means you'll have an easier time transporting items there in the first place, and it will be more convenient to check in regularly to see how things are selling.

3. **Ask about the terms.** Ask the owner or manager how the shop's consignment agreement works. What percentage does the consignment shop keep? A cut in the range of 50 to 75 percent is common. Are there any fees on top of that? Most shops do not charge a consignment fee, but if there is, it shouldn't be more than $5 to $10. Ask if the shop owner notifies consigners when a price is lowered, and inquire how your stuff will be displayed. Exposure equals sales potential.

4. **Get it in writing.** Make sure you have the terms of the consignment in writing, and that you get a concise but detailed receipt for whatever you give the shop.

money. The local readership may be easier to reach in other ways, and you just can't guarantee eyes on your ad. If you think this might work for you, though, you'll find a web address and phone number to post an ad at the beginning of the classified section in the publication you're looking at. *Penny Saver*, which claims to reach 11.2 million Americans, may be an option for you. It now has an online component as well, where you can place ads for free. If you see people reading it in your area, you may want to consider it.

Pawnshops

People are sometimes surprised that I'm not opposed to pawn-shops. That's because these shops are tightly regulated and most are reputable. With pawnshops, you get cash for an item and you are done with it. Your primary goal is to save time; your secondary goal is to profit financially.

This option might not be right for everything you want to sell, but it can be a good outlet for specific categories of items. For example, you would think that jewelry is a natural for a pawnshop sale, but pawnbrokers tend to grossly undervalue jewelry. Ultimately, silver and gold jewelry is usually melted down, and the pawnbroker is looking for the best price per ounce. He or she is unlikely to consider the value of a vintage

Tiffany piece. On the other hand, musical instruments (especially guitars), watches, and firearms are hot items in pawnshops. We called a pawnshop in the area to look at Mary's vinyl collection—I'd worked with the pawnbroker before and knew he used to own a record store. He offered Mary $1,000, which was amazing. She was happy with it, too. Be ready to negotiate to get the best price for any item you take to a pawnshop. If you're uncomfortable with haggling, ask someone you trust to deal with the pawnbroker on your behalf.

Auction Houses

Auctioning an item makes sense only if it is worth a reasonable amount in the open market. Your ten-year-old leather ottoman? Not auction material. Mary's grandfather clock? Perfect. Auctions can be held in local brick-and-mortar operations or online. I prefer local auction houses that have an online component, but not all of them do, and not all online operations are equal. It would be wonderful if you could have both an interested group of in-person bidders and a full-fledged online auction component. Unfortunately, I haven't found that type of house for general stuff and a general audience, only for large, high-end operations such as Sotheby's—which probably won't be interested in your coin collection. In my experience, if you

MATT'S FOUR FAILSAFE RULES FOR USING A PAWNBROKER

1. Be clear from the get-go that you are not pawning the item, you are selling it. Selling it means you do not want it back. Pawning means they will give you some cash now and you can come back and buy it for another price if it has not sold yet.
2. Understand what is appropriate for pawnbrokers. The smaller the item the better (say, jewelry, coins, smaller musical instruments, and firearms). They don't have the space for large possessions like furniture.
3. Know your price range. Be willing to walk away from the transaction if you feel that the pawnbroker is lowballing you and offering what you consider a ridiculous price.
4. Be ready for legal requirements. Because pawnshops are tightly regulated, the broker must take steps to ensure you actually own the items you want to sell. That can involve answering a series of questions and filling out paperwork.

can't have both local and virtual, it's better to go online only. That's what we chose for Mary's grandfather clock.

With an online auction house, sellers get the maximum exposure for large items and reach the target audience they're looking to sell to. An in-person auction attracts only the people in the room; a digital auction attracts people from all over the world. Seriously, I've seen things put on sale online in the United States and sold to buyers in Mongolia, Australia, and Ecuador. And remember that if you are trying to sell an item, you just need two people to be interested before the bidding starts. But also understand that the auction house is looking to make as much money as possible; if the item is likely to sell for under, say, $500, it will probably want a higher percentage of the sale.

I generally guide my clients to larger online auction houses. Two large ones are Everything But The House (EBTH) and MaxSold. I've found that these two companies offer much larger pools of bidders than other auction houses, and I've worked with them both for years. You might also find a reputable local auction house with a professional, polished operation. Get recommendations for local companies by asking friends, movers, senior living communities, antique shops, or upscale vintage stores in the area. Check the local company's website. Make sure it posts detailed listings and has pages on social media sites like Instagram and Facebook; features only good-quality, in-focus pictures; and has a website that is easy to use. Check out the National Auctioneers Association website for information about trusted local auction houses.

You'll want to do your homework when choosing an auction house. For brick-and-mortar auction houses, go to a few and see the typical crowd size they draw. The bigger the better. Then watch the actual auction. You want a crowd with a lot of bidders rather than just window shoppers.

MARY'S AUCTION

We opted for a seven-day auction for Mary's grandfather clock—that is, the listing was open to bids for a seven-day period. We took ten solid photos of Mary's clock and supplied the auction website with a detailed description of the item, too. In my experience, people sometimes get lazy at this point and take shabby photos or skimp on the details. Note everything in your item description: condition, manufacturer, type of wood or material it's made of, actual dimensions, age. Look for the craftsman signature or mark because that can distinguish your product, especially if you're dealing with savvy collectors or buyers. That was the case in Mary's auction; the person who created her clock turned out to be the key differentiator. Put in the extra legwork, because these things matter to your prospective buyers!

I was encouraged at the amount of attention Mary's clock got before the listing even went live on the site. Several people emailed questions and it was clear that a lot of potential buyers

MATT'S EIGHT TIPS FOR CHOOSING AN AUCTION HOUSE

1. Check out online auction houses—or online components of brick-and-mortar ones. You're not helping your cause if the company posts a blurry photo and a two-word description of your item on its website that attracts very little traffic. Is there an email registration or at least a sign-up on the website? Are the listings detailed and well written, with multiple, high-quality photographs? Is the website easy to navigate? Is bidding easy?

2. Ask how many unique bidders the auction house has each month. The number should be in the thousands.

3. Attend virtual or in-person auctions to judge how well the business conducts itself, how many potential bidders the company draws, and how the on-site or in-person bidding works.

4. Ask about marketing. Does the company send out email blasts, email newsletters, or other marketing? Does it advertise on sites like Facebook or Instagram or through Google?

5. Talk to the sales associate dedicated to particular categories, such as furniture or rare coins. Ask for an overview of the specifics, including how long the auction will last, how the house will market it, a range for what they think your item will bring in, what you need to do to en-

sure success, and shipping information. Online companies usually have all or much of this in writing on their
websites.

6. Ask the sales associate or auctioneer what reporting
you'll receive at the end of the sale process. Any reputable seller will give you a detailed report of every single
item that sold, what it sold for, and what its commissions
were. The good auction houses will automatically give
you this report, and many are required to by law. If they
don't offer this, don't work with them.

7. Before you sign an agreement with an auction house,
be absolutely certain you understand who will pay for
shipping (and the shipping speed specified), who is in-
suring the item and for how much, and what happens in
the case of a problem, such as the item going missing
after it's shipped to the buyer. You also want to determine how quickly you'll be paid. Most auction houses
don't cut your payment until the buyer's payment has
cleared the bank or credit card charge. My experience
is that payment can take from twenty-five to forty-five
days.

8. Once you settle on a company, there may be some room
to negotiate the percentage the house takes. It's usually
30 to 50 percent, commonly falling at 40 percent. That
sounds like a lot, but a quality company provides marketing, promotion, presentation, expertise, and reach that
you could never match on your own. It might even supply

professional-level photography services. Auction houses usually maintain a list of well-heeled clients whom they can alert to specific sales. A good house will know who is an avid stamp collector and who wants a heads-up when a rare baseball card comes up for auction. They will almost always also have a strong email list for marketing purposes. That's a big part of what makes these companies so attractive for declutterers and downsizers. I tell my clients that if you use a reputable company, your 60 percent cut from an auction usually translates to more money than you'd get by selling the item on your own.

were looking. Looking isn't the same as writing a check, of course, but it's always a good sign. We made sure to answer the questions quickly, politely, and comprehensively.

The early bids shocked me and Mary. Five days in, the bidding had reached $5,000. Suddenly, when her daughters heard of the bids on the clock, they all clamored that they wanted it! The daughters were teasing their mom, but in many families, that is the unfortunate response to finding out that a disregarded family heirloom actually has significant financial value. I've seen it cause rifts between siblings and a lot of bad feelings. Fortunately, Mary's daughters were happy their mom would get a little windfall. In any case, she was committed to the sale.

The last few hours of any auction are usually the make-or-break period and the most fun. If there is a lot of hidden interest, it will show itself. That's exactly what happened with Mary's clock. One bid after another flew in: $6,000, then $10,000, then $12,000. Higher and higher it went. With an hour left to go, the high bid stood at $20,000. I called Mary in disbelief as we watched the prices rise online. Twenty grand and still an hour to go.

The winning bid was just over $35,000. Even minus the 40 percent cut the auction house took, it was an enormous amount. I asked Mary if she would divide the money up among the kids. She laughed. "Heck, no. I'm going on a cruise!" When her daughters found out what she was going to do with the money, they were all for her plan. What they didn't know yet was they would all be going with her on that dream vacation.

Sales like this are happy surprises. With all my experience pricing and selling more than a dozen grandfather clocks, I'd never seen one take off like that. I felt good for Mary that it did. She avoided one of the key mistakes I've seen many declutterers and downsizers make: flip-flopping on the decision to sell. I've had clients who get stars in their eyes when they find out there is actual interest on the market in one of their heirlooms. Inevitably, there is this emotional urge to say, "Oh, it's valuable! I should hold on to it." I think that's a pretty human response. Instead, though, Mary did the right thing. When she couldn't bequeath the clock, she resigned herself to selling it and stuck to her decision.

Several days after the auction, Mary and I watched as the shipping company came in and packed up the grandfather clock. She didn't seem sad to see it go on the truck. She had done the smart thing; she had made peace with her decision.

Throughout this book, I've spoken about emotion a lot, but this chapter is more about the nuts and bolts than about dealing with your feelings. That's deliberate. Don't let emotions get in the way of your selling—if you do, you'll find a way to keep everything. Remember, you've already decided you don't want these items and you don't want to give them to your friends or family. So you have already taken emotion out of it. If you start to get emotional now, you will just end up holding on to the item rather than decluttering. Mary did it right: Once she made her decision, she stuck to it, regardless of the price her items garnered. In fact, she ended up paying a junk collector $100 to pick up her furniture—it just didn't make sense to even try to sell it. It was an easy spreadsheet decision.

Mary was fortunate in a lot of ways, not just in her determination and success in the auction. She knew what she wanted to do with her life, and what she wanted to do with her stuff. And not least, her living space was in great condition. But not everyone is in such a good position. In the next chapter we'll talk about how to clean properly, which is an essential component of the decluttering process.

STEP EIGHT
. . . .
Clean Up

JANICE CALLED ME IN 2014 to empty out her parents' home after they passed away. The house, in Ohio, had been vacant for several years, when her parents lived in Florida. Some belongings had already been sold and donated. Janice needed us to get rid of any leftover items and give the place a good deep clean before she put it up for sale.

Janice and her wife, Natasha, were there to greet us at one of the most impressive homes I'd ever seen. It was a big, fancy old brick house surrounded by large trees. The backyard led down to a ravine. Inside, the home had the original wood floors, ten-foot-high ceilings, and impressive arched doorways.

The problem was that the home's beauty was difficult to see. Virtually abandoned, the house was covered in years' worth of grime, dust, rust, and more than a few bugs.

"It looks like the morning after a two-week rock concert," Natasha said dryly.

Getting the house in shape for prospective buyers was one goal. Even more intriguing: We were tasked with finding valuable items that could be hidden anywhere. Janice explained that her father collected old train memorabilia and had amassed a lucrative stash of old engine parts, train schedules, and identification plates from steam engines. In previous eras, each train got a unique cast-iron ID plate, identifying the year, model type, and region in which it operated. These are collectors' items that now typically garner $1,000 to $2,000, although some of the unique ones from famous locomotives can be worth a lot more. Janice's father had told her about the plates many years ago, and he'd said he had twenty of them. But she hadn't lived in that house for decades, and despite searching in every nook and cranny when she initially decluttered, she hadn't found them. If we unearthed the full set of plates, she told my team, we'd be finding real history and making her a lot of money. I'd never seen my employees so excited to start the final cleanup. We got to work.

Once you've sorted through all your possessions and have sold, donated, given, or thrown away what you don't want, there is only the final physical cleanup to do before packing and moving (if you are moving, that is), which I go into in the next chapter. This is when you get it done—no more planning, just action. Yes, it can be dirty. Sometimes it can be unpleasant. But cleaning isn't only about scrubbing floors and cabinets, just like packing isn't just about stuffing belongings in boxes. This process is about respecting the past but also ensuring the smoothest transition between your old life and the new life you're beginning.

You can find an enormous sense of satisfaction once rooms get cleaned out. But there can also be some melancholy, as the door closes on one part of our life even as another begins. We're sweeping away not just dirt and dust but the past and its challenges. We're cleaning out the powerful memories that have formed the people we've become.

Rest assured, though: You're bringing those with memories with you, wherever you're going. And you're bringing the stories that go with the memories, too.

SAFETY PRECAUTIONS

On a bright fall morning, I arrived at Janice's parents' house with my team of three, who were all wearing steel-toed boots, masks, gloves, and safety goggles. One of my employees, Jamal, was decked out in a full hazmat suit.

Janice was amused at our outfits. "There isn't a nuclear spill in there," she joked.

But honestly, none of us knew what was in there. I've cleaned some of the messiest homes in the United States—including homes of extreme hoarders—where I learned one simple lesson: Never assume a home (and particularly its attic and basement) is safe. Treat every house as if it were dangerous. When you declutter and clean, you unearth all sorts of things. Some of them—like the train plates we hoped to find—are delightful surprises. Others—like the sizable collection of dead squirrels I once found in a home—are not. Some of the things you'll find are items once considered safe but are now categorized as hazards, like fertilizer or mercury. You might think you know your living space. But even the best-kept homes sometimes attract mice, ants, roaches, and other unwelcome creatures. Add in some clutter and filth and the creatures become bolder and more numerous. Alas, the vermin and insects are some of the easiest dangers you could encounter. Before you even enter the house or wherever you're clearing out, you want to take precautions.

- **Mask up.** You probably don't know that, by some estimates, more than 90 percent of homes in America are lined with fiberglass insulation, which can cause skin irritation and breathing difficulties. Insulation is often exposed in basements and attics, so be extra careful there. But whenever you're cleaning out a home, always wear a mask. Use the tips we learned during the COVID-19 pandemic. The N95 masks, which block at least 95 percent of small airborne particles (hence the name), will help keep you safe. When my team is around a lot of chemicals, paints, or dirt, we go through three masks a day per person. If N95s are scarce, use the KN95s or P100s, or double up your paper or cloth masks.
- **Don gloves.** From paper cuts to stray rusty nails to dangerous chemicals, your hands are vulnerable to any number of hazards while you're cleaning and packing. We use coated nitrile or polyurethane-coated gloves because they're easy to use, disposable, and inexpensive, and you can grab small things. Most big box hardware stores have ten-packs of the polyurethane-coated gloves for about $10.

- **Wear safety glasses.** There are often airborne particulates floating around, along with dust and other stuff. In attics and basements particularly, nails and wood chips can protrude from the ceiling. Items can fall from shelves at the best of times. I buy the multipack of goggles at the hardware store. Wipe them clean at the end of each day and reuse them the next. Even better, when you're done with them, you can usually toss them into your recycling bin. I'd estimate one or two pairs per person for the entire job. If you normally wear eyeglasses, just put the safety glasses over them.

- **Invest in safe shoes.** Don't neglect your feet. You want your shoes to be leather and, if possible, steel-toed. You want the sole and the toe to be as strong as possible, because if you're carrying anything heavy or pulling things down from higher spaces, something will invariably fall on your toes. No sneakers or sandals. As comfortable as your flip-flops are, they will not protect you. Spending $50 on a pair of boots is better than a trip to the hospital to fix a broken foot. I've found affordable safety boots at Walmart and on Amazon. If you are going to wear them a lot, like I do, I prefer a nice pair of slide-on Blundstones or Dr. Martens.

- **Watch your step.** I've seen it many times: Someone puts a foot on an attic floor, breaks through the flimsy material, and crashes into the room below. Attics don't have proper flooring to sustain the weight of an adult; it's not what they were built for. Put down plywood across the beams before you walk through an attic. That might sound cumbersome, but it's the only way to reliably prevent accidents. If using plywood is impossible, walk on the wooden beams—but be extra careful where you put your feet.

- **Never walk across the top of boxes in the attic,** basement, garage, or anywhere else! I learned this the hard way. When I moved to Georgia, I climbed onto the boxes on the back of the moving truck to inspect the job the movers had done. I slipped off and fell about six feet down onto my driveway. I broke my wrist, and it took months to fully heal. My newest rule of thumb: If you start to wonder whether you are too old to be doing something safely, you probably are.

- **Watch for mold.** Another reason you'll want gloves and masks is that you might come across mold, which congregates in dark and damp places. If you see dark spots on the wall or smell mildew, call in a professional mold remediation expert—don't touch it and don't try to clean it yourself. Mold is dangerous, potentially making you and your family sick. The pros aren't as expensive as you might think. And it may be covered under your homeowners' or renters' insurance; ask your expert. Call a mold mitigation specialist and ask for a free estimate.

DANGEROUS FINDS

Janice had warned us about old chemicals, big engine parts, a fifty-five-gallon drum of oil in the backyard, and the usual pests and dirt that find their way into homes. There are other dangers to be mindful of when decluttering, however, and they include not just the environment you're working in but the items you find. Even the cleanest of houses can be a minefield of hazards. Please call a local expert if you come across something dangerous.

- **Stashes of old fireworks might be exciting, but they are a fire hazard that can take an eye out.** Please resist the urge of putting on a big show for your neighbors, and don't sell them, either, since you can't be sure of their safety. Completely submerge and soak the fireworks in water for twenty minutes, double bag them in plastic, and then throw them away in the regular trash.
- **A lot of our clients find guns or ammunition.** Especially among older generations, we find hand grenades from the

Korean and Vietnam Wars. Make sure you never pick up a gun, even if you consider yourself skilled with firearms. Assume that it's loaded. Never point it at someone. If the owner isn't around, contact a local firearms specialist to help you dispose of it. In my company, when we come upon a firearm, we put our hands up and walk away. Either the owner handles it alone or I call in a professional to take it away. A professional gun handler is often an off-duty police officer or someone from a local gun shop. A local gun shop or police department will tell you who to call. Assume there will be a fee for this, but it's worth it in the long run. There are about fifteen thousand accidental gun deaths in the United States every year, so this rule is no joke.

- **Oil-based paints are considered hazardous waste.** If you've got more than a half gallon of paint, please consider donating it to Habitat for Humanity. Most cities will allow you to dry the cans out before you dispose of them, provided that you do so in the right manner. You can either get a special paint-drying product at a hardware store, or use a one-to-one ratio of cat litter.

- **Look out for medications.** There are particular ways to get rid of leftover prescriptions, specifically narcotics. You cannot simply throw them in the trash since someone could find them at the dump and take them. Do not flush your old medications down the toilet. Flushing them or pouring them down the drain contaminates the water. Check with your local pharmacy, fire and police departments, or the Drug Enforcement Administration website to find the proper disposal program. Don't give them to your nephew who is taking a year off to find himself, even if he asks politely!

- **Needles, syringes, and lancets must go in special sharps containers.** Anytime you are helping clean out a home, ask everyone who lives there if there are any needles in the home. If so, call your doctor's office or local hospital to see if you can drop them off. If you put sharps in a trash bag, they can poke through and harm anyone who picks up the bag. If someone in your home is diabetic, don't always assume the orange caps are sealed tightly. When cleaning up a home where a person with diabetes has lived, remove the needles safely. You can order sharps containers online, and sometimes hospitals give them away for free. If you are cleaning up a house that has lots of hypodermic needles, wear needle-safe gloves. They're about a hundred bucks but worth the cost.

- **Chemicals for cleaning and pest control can be dangerous.** They're usually in the garage or the basement, and they're a powder or liquid substance that are sometimes unmarked. Assume that unlabeled products are dangerous. Ask your local health department how to properly dispose of these; most cities have a special place at the dump for disposal. That's what we did with unrecognizable, unmarked chemicals we found in small containers in a pantry in Janice's parents' house. They were probably used on trains, but since none of us were chemical engineers, we couldn't be sure. Jamal's hazmat suit came in handy as he escorted the weird-looking chemicals to the dump and handed them over to the pros.

- **For other medical waste, like adult diapers, colostomy bags, and bloody bandages, call the local health department.** Understand your options for disposal, because most of these items cannot be thrown away at the city dump. If there is a large enough volume, call Stericycle, Clean Earth, Cantel Medical, or another medical waste disposal company. They'll be able to handle all the heavy lifting and navigate the local disposal laws.

- **Finding a deceased animal is all too common in my work.** Whether you find a possum in the attic, a squirrel in the fireplace, or your favorite cat lovingly buried in the backyard, most localities have rules about how to dispose of animals properly. Most of the time, you're going to have to go to a pet cremation center. If there is a hole in the roof and the attic is filled with animals like possum or raccoons and/or their excrement, turn around, get out, and call a professional disaster restoration or mold remediation company like ServiceMaster or First Onsite.

FINDING MONEY

After we did an initial sweep looking for potential dangers, the first thing we did inside Janice's parents' house—even before we began cleaning—was go looking for the plates. Who wouldn't hunt around for a hidden treasure potentially worth tens of thousands of dollars? As we ran around the home scrounging around, Janice said we looked like kids hunting for Easter eggs. I thought the plates might be in the basement with the other remnants of the trains, but no luck. My colleague headed for the attic and came up empty. Jamal checked under the bedroom mattress—there was no way someone would hide old plaques there, but he wanted to be sure. We didn't find what we were looking for in the bedroom, but we did find about $100 in coins and bills scattered around.

In fact, if you are decluttering and cleaning, you're likely to find cash—but it won't be where you expect it. When was the last time you looked inside the tank in the back of your parents' toilet? That may seem like an odd question, but it's one of the first places we usually look when we're hired to clean out houses after a parent or grandparent dies. People of a certain age are notorious for creating secret hiding places for money, so finding their treasure troves after they're gone requires patience and a little detective work. People who grew up during the Depression era understandably don't trust banks, so they often hid money because it felt safer than the alternative. As you go through the house, have a glass fishbowl handy, because you're going to find loose change, and you need to put it somewhere. When change hits a glass bowl, it makes an unforgettable sound that gets you excited and keeps up the momentum. If you are a helper, every time the homeowners hear that sound, they are hearing that they can trust you.

Hiding places are unique to the house and to the individual, so the best way to uncover your family member's secret stash is to ask them while they are still around to tell you. Even if they lived very modestly, older generations took great pride in living frugally and saving as much as they could. In fact, the ones who never talked about money usually are the ones who we discover have the most hidden. Only once you're sure that there's no cash squirreled away in random parts of the home can you confidently begin to throw things out while you're cleaning.

TOP TEN SECRET HIDING PLACES

These are the most common places we've found money over the years. Check them all before you conclude that a home is cashless:

1. Toilet tanks. There's plenty of room in the toilet's water tank for a jar or some other watertight container stuffed with cash or jewelry. And while you're in there, make sure nothing's taped to the inside of the lid.
2. Freezers. Cold, hard cash is more than a cliché. We've found everything from credit cards to gold coins frozen inside blocks of ice, and plastic zipper bags filled with cash.
3. Pantries. Look inside every cereal box, flour bag, and coffee can. Pour out the contents if necessary so you can see what's at the bottom.
4. Bookshelves. Yes, you want to check for those hollowed-out Bibles and dictionaries that you can buy online. But you also have to shake out every book on the shelf. We've found everything from $100 bills to dividend checks from Fortune 50 companies in the amount of $2,500 stashed between the pages of paperbacks and hardbacks. Grab each book by the spine and shake it left to right. Any cash will drop out quickly. I recommend shaking every book in the house if time allows.

5. Under the floorboards. This is a common place to hide valuables, especially in older houses. Check for loose boards under throw rugs, new nails that look out of place, and loose edges around wall-to-wall carpets. I'm not recommending you pull up all the flooring, but if a section looks different, check it out.

6. Old trunks. Steamer trunks used in World War II had special compartments built into them for wives to pack mementos for their husbands who were going off to fight. Check under the lining and look for a false bottom. The secret compartment is usually on the right-hand side of the back of the trunk near the bottom.

7. Closets. You have to go through every piece of clothing and every box. We've found hundreds of thousands of dollars in shoeboxes and cigar boxes and inside the pockets and lining of old jackets. Wear gloves, because while you might not find money, I can guarantee you will find used tissues in those pockets.

8. Drawers. We've found envelopes full of cash or other valuables taped to the bottom or the back of just about every type of furniture, but chests of drawers offer unique hiding places. Women's vanities usually have at least one drawer with a false bottom to hide the good jewelry.

9. The backyard. It's not just something you see in the movies; people really did bury canning jars filled with rolled-up $20 bills in the yard. Look for turned dirt or dis-

placed grass, and for items that aren't buried too deeply, try a metal detector. If you've heard rumors that Dad hid stuff in the backyard and the metal detector pings, you might want to start digging.

10. Birthday cards and church envelopes. People often load these with cash and then forget to mail them, or they receive them and forget to open them. Open every single card you find. If you are in a hurry, hold the envelope up to the light and you can often see what's inside.

HOW TO CLEAN

For even the smallest cleaning job, the right supplies make the task easier, quicker, and better. Janice didn't have much on hand beyond a mop, bleach, and Clorox Clean-Up—we checked under the sink and in the laundry room and closets for anything—but we generally bring our own anyway. It sounds like a hassle to get a laundry list of products together, but you're going to want all these items before you get started. They won't cost more than $100 altogether, but they'll save you tons of energy. If you have to keep stopping and going to the store to get more stuff, or working with products that don't do the job, your momentum slows and the job takes longer.

- **Rags.** I rip apart T-shirts, old towels, and other thin, soft fabrics to make rags to wipe everything down.
- **Microfiber towels and paper towels.** They both serve a purpose. Many products that are great for cleaning are not so great for the environment, including paper towels. If you prefer paper towels, look for the recycled bamboo ones. Most people are using microfiber towels. They clean better than paper towels and are proven to remove 99 percent of the bacteria on a surface. You can also use them longer and they won't leave any residue on glass or shiny surfaces. I also like them because you can throw the dirty rags in a bucket as you clean, wash them all at night, and use them again the next day. In my experience, Norwex works well and holds up after repeated uses, but there are lots of good generic brands on the market.
- **Scrubbing tools.** Have on hand a stainless steel scrubbing pad, a toothbrush for tough spots, and many sponges and scouring pads. I now use the recycled coconut shell sponges, simply because my wife makes me, no other reason.
- **Natural cleaning products.** Seventh Generation, Clorox Green Works, and Simple Green are among my favorite choices. Use a microfiber rag and a natural spray cleaner instead of paper towels. Tea tree oil is God's gift to cleaning, so when you see that as a main ingredient, you are

good to go. Conversely, bleach and other strong chemical-based products can wreak havoc over time on both home surfaces and the environment. Those disinfecting wipes are great for killing all bacteria. Believe it or not, some bacteria is good and you don't want to kill them all. Plus, most people don't use those wipes properly. Read the directions: They probably need to stay wet on the surface for several minutes to work. Some disinfectant chemicals can also trigger asthma and allergies. Disinfectant wipes are best for cleaning up after sick kids or washing raw chicken from surfaces, but use them correctly and avoid them otherwise.

- **A big, strong broom and a large dustpan.** When these basics are cracked or broken, they make everything else more difficult.

- **Thick garbage bags.** You're going to want clear plastic bags and dark black ones. The clear bags are for donating and recycling, while the black bags are for trash. Following this color code helps you track what's what. Opt for the three-millimeter-thick bags, which are durable. The common one- or two-millimeter bags are fine for your leaves and yard waste, but you'll want stronger bags that can hold books and other heavy materials. I like the big fifty-five-gallon bags for moving. They generally come in twenty-five-count boxes. I usually get five to six boxes per house. Open them as you need them so you can return the boxes you don't use.

- **Trash cans and recycling bins.** These are indispensable to carry things in and out of the house.
- **Pocketknife or box cutter.** Using kitchen knives to open boxes has led to many a sliced hand.
- **Rake.** For really messy homes, you may need to rake the carpet before you vacuum it. This loosens up buried debris, from food crumbles to pet hair. Vacuums suck up the surface stuff, but rakes get the down-and-dirty material.
- **Vacuum.** My go-to brands are Miele, Oreck, and Simplicity. The super-popular vacuums with exciting names and great pitchmen aren't always the most effective. Do your research before buying a vacuum. Check out all the reviews and make sure you choose one that is powerful, long-lasting, and can meet all your health needs. Also make sure the vacuum is strong enough to handle airborne allergens and, if you have a pet, fur. Remember to change out the bags and filters often.

If you're looking for help hauling away last-minute items, I've used and can recommend three companies. They have a national reach and are licensed, bonded, insured, and trustworthy. I promise you that, whatever situation you're in and whatever items you have left over, they've seen it before. You'll pay a premium, but it may be worth it.

- 1-800-GOT-JUNK?
- College Hunks Hauling Junk & Moving
- Junk King

Once everything was out of Janice's parents' house, we got to work cleaning the same way that I like to begin decluttering: in a small area where we can quickly see a difference and feel a sense of accomplishment. All four members of my team washed down the kitchen, from the dust-covered hardwood floors to the grimy fridge to the drain-clogged sink. The pantry had years-old pastas, junk food, and cans of vegetables piled up. We looked for expiration dates and put aside for the food bank anything that was still good. Within an hour, the kitchen looked far better, giving us a boost of encouragement as we continued on our mission. Of course, four people are faster than one, but even a concentrated solo effort can quickly make a good dent in a messy home.

I've developed shortcuts and hacks in every stage of decluttering, and cleaning is no different. Here are some other cleaning tips:

- **In many areas, public waste collectors** are allowed to take only the bin and one or two additional bags of garbage at a time. If you have large items or more than a few bags, try offering to buy them lunch and tipping them an extra $20 each—they're much likelier to help you out with your requests once you've taken care of them.

- **Recycle anything you can.** But the materials you're able to recycle vary widely depending on your state, your city, and sometimes even your county. Call your local recycling company—you'd be surprised what you can deliver to it. In addition, whoever picks up the recycling at your curb may know of other resources. Many things in your home can be recycled, but you have to do the research and legwork to get it there. Also call the local dump—many of them have drop-off areas for lots of sorted plastics. I once tried to throw away an old TV in California, but that state considers such electronics to be e-waste, separated from other trash. Just know that your geographic location matters when recycling. Take the extra minute and call to find out the best way to recycle your items.

- **I'm not big on steam cleaning your carpets by yourself with store-bought cleaners,** because it's a job that requires skill and training to do properly. When cleaning out homes, I constantly find mediocre steam cleaners that were used one time and then put back in the garage because they were deemed ineffective. The professional steam cleaners you can rent are much more powerful. Indeed, you can rent steam cleaners as well as industrial vacuums and special cleaning equipment from your local hardware or even grocery store. If hiring a professional carpet cleaner, be very clear on how many rooms you want cleaned to get a reliable estimate.

- **For bathroom showers and tiles,** there is no better scrubber than the Dremel Versa cleaning tool. It cleans tile, glass, grout, and ceramics. You can get it online or at any home improvement store. Any good all-purpose or bathroom cleaning foam will also do. Clogged drain? If you need more than one bottle of drain cleaner, call the plumber.

YOUR FINAL DEEP CLEAN

If you hear a real estate agent say "broom sweep," it means exactly that: All you have to do is sweep the house clean. But a deep clean or construction clean is what I'll discuss here. This is the last and final powerful clean of the entire house. You want to get up high with a broom to get the cobwebs out of the corners, brush the dust off the tops of the fans, and wipe every corner of the windows and baseboards. Use a sturdy stool to reach the backs of the cabinet shelves. Run the broom across the top of the baseboards and dump the bugs out of the glass bowls on the light fixtures. I'm big on broom-sweeping the entire home first, top to bottom, finishing with the floor. Sweep the steps from the top down. Once every surface has been cleaned, then you can clean the floors. The old days of using the mop are done. The tools I use are the Swiffer, Bona, and Bissell. You'll be fine with any of them.

If you are going to do the windows, this is the one place I don't think about the environment. I've just never found an all-natural cleaner that works well. I'm big on an aerosol cleaner called Sprayway, but Windex is another option. You may have learned that the key to leaving no streaks is newspaper. It's true, although if you don't like newsprint on your hands, a good micro-fiber cloth will be adequate. For outdoor windows that are really filthy, I'd stick to newspaper.

Lastly, I like to replace the light bulbs and the batteries in the smoke detectors, if a client is moving, just because it's a nice thing to do for the next owner.

If this seems like too much, don't be afraid to ask your professional house cleaner to come out and give you an estimate for a full house deep clean. Expect it to be two to three times your normal monthly cleaning rate and take up to six hours.

A FINAL LOOK

Once you've gotten everything out of the house and cleaned it top to bottom, grab a garbage bag and do another walk-through of the space. I guarantee you will find items, often trash. I've told my employees for years: When you think you are done, there is inevitably still one more bag of trash left in the home, behind closed doors, in closets, and in the back of built-in drawers. Especially if you're contractually required to leave behind a spotless home for future tenants or homeowners, you'll want to do a final sweep to ensure that you're meeting your obligations—some management companies and landlords love to find any slipup to hold on to security deposits or claim breach of contract.

After we'd finished cleaning Janice's parents' home, we were disappointed that we hadn't found the locomotive plates but satisfied with a job well done. The beauty of the house really shone through in ways it hadn't just a few days earlier. Each of us carrying a bag, we went through for our final walk, determined to look through every corner of that home for any trace of trash.

About five minutes in, I heard a yell from Jamal in the basement. We ran down and saw him grinning as he held a dusty plaque nearly covered in gooey dust. He'd looked under the last step of the basement staircase and noticed a ratty old cloth. He pulled it over and we all heard a loud gratifying sound of two plaques hitting each other. Even in the dim room, Jamal's careful eye had spotted the old cloth holding the plaque. And as we watched, he revealed more black cloths—twenty-one in total. Each one contained a plaque commemorating a different train. He held them up like they were pieces of gold—which they basically were. We immediately videoconferenced Janice and Natasha, and their eyes widened when we showed them the hidden treasure. They eventually sold the collection of plaques for more than $60,000. To find anything that valuable is exciting, but to be honest, the quest was more exhilarating than the money.

Most important, of course, Janice was able to sell her parents' home in excellent condition. We had cleaned well. While we were working, she got more emotional than she expected. That happens often at this phase, because this is when the reality of the decluttering process is physically visible. The implications of what you're doing—literally leaving behind certain things, choosing to shed old skins—become apparent. It's best to feel these emotions, to let them wash through you. The way you are feeling is the way you are feeling—you don't need to judge it, nor try to avoid it. Just be with it. And remind yourself that you're creating a better version of yourself by creating circumstances that are better suited to the one you want to lead.

This stage, like the others, can be very emotional, since it's the undeniable end of one season in your life, even while it marks the beginning of a new one. Packing and moving are the final steps in the journey for some of you and the beginning of a new life, and they are simultaneously challenging but also thrilling stages. I'll turn there next.

STEP NINE

· · · · · · · · · ·

Move Forward

MOVING IS GENERALLY LISTED AS one of the top five stress-
ors in life. In my twenty-plus years in the decluttering and
downsizing industry, I've never had a client who found it easy.
Even those who are excited about moving can find the process
gut-wrenching. You'd think, with all my experience, with all
my years in the business, with my moving literally thousands of
clients, my move in 2020 would be an exception. But as you read
earlier in this book, you'd be wrong.

Here's the good news: Because I had fallen in love with a
minimalist, I had no choice but to get rid of roughly 75 percent
of the stuff I owned, so moving should have been easier and less
expensive than expected. Once again, it was a spreadsheet issue:

Having less stuff saved me money on everything from packing materials to the size of the moving truck needed to haul our stuff.

Here's the bad news: Although my move was relatively simple, the downsizing was still tumultuous and draining. Luckily, I learned a lot in my process, and I'll pass on that advice to you. Decluttering or downsizing is a journey, a trip of acceptance— and sometimes you take some detours on that journey. That's okay. All that matters is that you reach your destination, physically and emotionally.

TIMELINE

Once I made the decision to move, the first thing I needed to do was set a timeline. Because we were in the height of the coronavirus quarantine, my boys and I were already spending all our time at home. That gave us more time to focus on decluttering and packing. In my experience, allocating four or five months maximum for the packing and moving and unpacking—from start to finish—should be plenty.

But whatever your timeline, set a deadline or you'll never get it done. I've heard horror stories from former clients who moved into new homes but drove back and forth to clean up previous homes for years because they didn't commit to the effort and just get it done. It took me years to realize how important it is to wrap this up and not let it drag on. You might not be able to devote yourself to this full-time the way I did when my dad died, but set up times when you'll do it, and establish a time limit. Deciding, decluttering, downsizing, and cleaning can take substantial time and require difficult choices. But packing and moving are not themselves time-consuming. It's easy to keep delaying the process so that the moving date keeps receding. The hardest part of packing up and moving isn't the work itself—it's the emotional upheaval. The best way to deal with those strong feelings is to face them directly. Stretching out the difficulties only sets back the date when you can begin your new life and create new memories, which is what ultimately resolves any lingering feelings of doubt and discomfort you have about moving.

YOUR CHECKLIST FOR PACKING AND MOVING

If you can afford to, you might decide to hire a move manager. That person or company will do everything for you, from getting the boxes and packing to hiring the movers to setting up your new place and even putting fresh linens on your bed. (To find a good move manager, look back at Step Three.) I also recommend hiring professional movers, and paying them to do the packing. Of course, not everyone can afford that luxury, and many people just prefer to DIY. If you're in that category, here's a checklist of what you need to do:

- Get packing supplies, which I list below.
- Call your homeowners' or renters' insurance carrier to get your valuables covered during the move. Ask your agent what you need. You may have to ask for a separate line item for an object you want covered. It's worth paying an extra $100 to insure a $10,000 painting. Make sure to itemize and take pictures of your most prized possessions before the move in case something breaks and you have to involve insurance companies. Remember that the software FairSplit is an easy way to inventory your home.
- If you're moving out of or into a building with an elevator, schedule your move with the management. Many buildings specify times for tenants to use elevators while moving and may stipulate parking and entrances for trucks and movers.
- Have the internet and landline phone, if you have one, installed ahead of time if possible. It's nice to have the TV and WiFi when you get there. It also keeps the kids busy.

- Find a moving company. There are a lot of companies out there, so see the section below on ways to make sure you get a good one. Or if you're DIY, rent a truck.
- Say last goodbyes.
- Take photos of each room.
- Unpack.
- Recycle boxes.
- Live blissfully ever after. (That'll be a future book!)

PACKING SUPPLIES

Here's what you're going to need to start packing:

- **Boxes.** I prefer regular old cardboard boxes. They're easy to write on. Expect to need at least sixty boxes per two-bedroom house, and another twenty for every additional bedroom or office. If you have an attic or basement, add another forty boxes. If you're short for time but long on cash, you can buy good boxes at a big box hardware store, storage unit place, or online in bulk. But if you have the time, you can go to any store and ask for empty boxes. Grocery stores are especially good targets because they move through merchandise so swiftly. Except for packing glass, I stay away from liquor stores because the boxes are so small. If you pack your entire house with liquor boxes, you'll be moving thousands of small boxes instead of hundreds of regular-size ones. You will be exhausted. You can also invest in specific cardboard boxes that will safely transport art or flat-screen televisions. They can be purchased at an art supply store or any home improvement store. Wherever you get your boxes, be sure you recycle them or give them away when you're done. I often give mine away on a local Buy Nothing Facebook group. Don't worry if you have too many boxes; you can always recycle them. Keeping all the boxes after you have moved is not a good way to start a new, less cluttered life.

If you are environmentally conscious, you can find companies that rent out reusable plastic bins. The company drops them off at your old place and picks them up at your new destination for the next customer. While they're better for the environment, they can be expensive, and you've got to unpack everything immediately. Sometimes a mix of both plastic and cardboard boxes is good.

- **Tape gun and tape.** Get at least one tape gun for each person helping with the move. Splurge on a steel tape gun; the plastic ones break fairly quickly. Estimate ten rolls of tape for a two-bedroom house. Add another two rolls for each additional room, and four for a basement or attic. Go with good packing or shipping tape, because it's the sturdiest and you can write on it. I generally use 3M packing tape. Don't scrimp; this tape is holding all your possessions safely and securely. A good taping job is indispensable to a successful move—especially long-distance moves.

- **Packing paper.** For most dishes, I recommend rolls of packing paper you can get at any hardware store. If you have newspapers sitting around, you can use them, but the ink from them does get the dishes dirty. Use bubble wrap, available at any hardware store (and sometimes dollar stores), for the fragile items.

- **Crates.** If you have sculptures or framed art, crates are available at specialty art stores or online. Don't skimp on these—get one for every valuable piece of art you own. They might even be required for your insurance. If you're hiring movers, you may need to pay extra, but an additional $250 to crate a painting worth $10,000 is money well spent.

- **Markers.** Sharpies are good, strong markers that you're going to need to write on everything from cardboard boxes to tape. I like to have two black ones and one silver Sharpie for each person. The silver ones are for black plastic bags and can help you mark trash from recyclables. The black ones are for everything else. Have two or three of these in your pocket every morning. And yes, keep them in your pocket. Once you put them down, you'll never find them again.

- **Blankets or pads.** These are a must for moving furniture and large items. If you are hiring professional movers, they will have the blankets or pads. If you're moving yourself, you can often rent them at a storage company, or purchase them from a hardware store or online. I have also bought and sold my blankets on Facebook Marketplace or Craigslist after using them. For a two-bedroom house, figure twenty blankets. Throw in another ten for each additional room.

- **Plastic trash bags, black and clear.** While you're packing up, even though you swore you were done sorting, I promise you are going to find stuff to donate, recycle, and trash, and that's what these bags are for. Black is for trash; clear is for donate. Put the recycled stuff straight into your recycle bin.

- **Mattress covers.** Most objects will be fine when covered with just blankets, but mattresses need special covering to keep them, because even a little dirt or water on them will make them unhygienic. Two separate one-time-use bags will be necessary if you are moving or storing a mattress and a box spring, but the bags are recyclable. Tape the end of the bag shut so dirt doesn't get in it during moving. Also, don't use these bags as the handle, because they will tear. Have an extra bag to put over the torn one if you are storing the mattress more than a few days. I'm a germaphobe, so I personally get two for each mattress and one for the box spring.

- **Tarps.** We often do a lot of sorting outside, and moving trucks have been known to leak. Tarps will keep the items safe and protected. I get about eight of these, at least six by eight feet, for every move. Place them on top of the boxes in the truck in case of rain.

- **Hand trucks.** You'll want dollies, those hand trucks that you can load up with boxes, appliances, or small pieces of furniture to carry up ramps and stairs. Try to have two dollies for each move. Any more than two will just create a traffic jam in your home and on the truck. Some hardware stores let you rent them by the day.

- **Water.** Packing is hard and sometimes emotional work. You've got to stay hydrated. You don't need any hardcore energy drinks, but each person should be drinking at least eight ounces of water—bottled, tap, just plain water— every few hours. You might think it's ridiculous to put on a list of supplies, but I can't tell you how many people I've seen get overheated during a move. This is strenuous work, and few of us are in good enough shape to be professional movers.

DO THE PACKING MATH

Over the years, I've seen countless people throw everything they own into boxes haphazardly and then wonder why they need such a big truck to move their stuff. Pack efficiently, and your belongings arrive intact to your new home. Pack poorly, and your stuff could shift and break. The best way to avoid these pitfalls is to treat packing like a game of Tetris: You want to pack items tightly and minimize space inside the boxes and bags. Arrange things so they fit together snugly. This is essentially a geometry problem, and the more math you do up front, the less you'll have to later to calculate how much money you lost in damaged goods during the move.

Make sure you understand where your personal insurance starts and stops. Most of us assume our items are covered inside the home we are moving from, and the stuff is covered by the mover's insurance from the point it gets on the truck to when they unpack it at your final destination. You want your items covered in your new home the day before you move.

HIRING MOVERS

For my move to Georgia, I booked some trusted friends at a local moving company. Given my experience, it was tempting to try and move myself. But really, nobody over the age of forty should be moving a lot of stuff, and nobody of any age should be moving furniture unless they have to for financial reasons. Moving is an easy way to suffer injuries, some of which can last a lifetime. If you can, please hire professionals. It's not worth trying to save a few bucks when the possible cost is a bad back for the next forty years.

How to sift through the moving companies out there and find the most reputable?

- **Get three estimates.** Book two to three companies for in-home estimates. Decline over-the-phone estimates. On-site is the only way movers can assess the job.
- **Get written, concrete estimates and an explanation of how the companies calculate charges.** But do understand

that the estimators can't see every corner in the attic or every box in the top of your closet. They can only get close. An estimate is exactly that: an educated guess as to how much it will cost. Understand that it could be up to 10 percent over what they think it's going to cost. Ask if there are any add-on charges that could be tacked on later, including payment for extra help, materials, or travel time. Most movers have a printed sheet with that information.

- **Are the companies you're considering licensed, bonded, and insured?** These are *the* key factors separating legitimate moving companies from start-ups run by college students. If a mover drops your nineteenth-century Italian vase in the middle of the street, will his company's insurance cover it? If not, don't even think about working with him. Ask to see the moving company's certificate of insurance, which provides proof of coverage.

- **If you're moving to another state or country, does your moving company have insurance there?** Your moving company needs insurance in the places you're moving to and from. If you're moving from Ohio to Missouri but your moving company is only insured in Ohio, you're in trouble if something breaks while unloading or unpacking in Missouri.

- **Do they use moving pads?** Professional moving companies use floor pads to protect your home from damage. A dropped appliance can cause a costly crack in a new $30,000 maple hardwood floor, and the movers would be held responsible. If the company you're interviewing doesn't use pads, find another company.

- **How many clients have they had?** Explain your situation to them and ask if they've worked with clients in similar circumstances. If they've done less than twenty moves, they haven't been in business long enough to trust them with your belongings.

- **Ask for references.** Then call those references. You should also check each company's Better Business Bureau ratings and the Google and Yelp reviews as well.

PLANNING THE LOGISTICS

If you're moving across town, you can probably pack and move in the same day. Because I was moving to a different state, our beds were packed in the truck overnight.

The goal for everyone is to keep it as stress-free as possible. So for children and pets, pack what they need to spend the night somewhere else—toiletries, medications, a change of clothes, a teddy bear, cat food and litter. If you can spend the night with friends or relatives, this is the time to call in favors. If they can't stay elsewhere, have enough entertainment to keep the kids busy.

Be prepared for things to break. No one intends for things to break, but they do. Usually, it's something small but important that gets cracked or shatters. Being aware that it will happen will make it easier to accept when it inevitably does. What matters is that the irreplaceable and valuable items aren't among the broken stuff. If your life would significantly change for the worse if an item broke, then you should probably move it yourself.

There are factors to consider if you're moving on your own:

- If you live in a suburban or urban area, try to move on a weekday. If there's no garage or loading zone, parking can be difficult.
- Look to see the distance from the truck to the entrance. A ramp will help if there's an uneven or hilly three-hundred-foot walkway to the door. Most rental trucks have ramps built in, but check to be sure.
- If it rains, is there a covered place to unload the truck? Moving in the rain is always difficult, but if you're par-

tially covered, you can minimize the damage and discomfort.

DOT YOUR I's AND CROSS YOUR T's

I helped Michelle declutter and move a few years ago. She had
multiple sclerosis and used a wheelchair, so my team spent
much time working closely with her to pack the stuff from her
two-room cottage. She was meticulous about every aspect of
the move, finding the best places to sell and donate her stuff,
making lists of what to keep and where it would go in her new
place. She obtained layouts of her new space and measured furniture. She was so well prepared that my team let her do a majority of the work we would normally handle. We had everything
ready to go the day before the move, with the truck packed up
and the next day set aside for the haul. I asked Michelle about
the parking at her new building. She wasn't sure, so I called the
new community's management company.

They'd had extensive conversations with Michelle, the
manager told me, but Michelle didn't in fact have an apartment
reserved! She'd never signed a contract. We had been so impressed with all her planning that we had failed to follow up

with her new place. This intelligent and careful individual had overlooked something so fundamental as making sure she had a place to live!

Fortunately, the company had an apartment available in the building. The measurements weren't the same as the one Michelle had planned for, which caused us more work. But we salvaged the situation. It was a good lesson: If you aren't careful, it's easy to miss vital components of this work. And another good lesson: Make sure you have a home ready to move to when you pack up the truck!

LAST GOODBYES

As soon as I decided to move to Georgia, I thought about how to say my goodbyes to friends and family members who lived nearby. As I mentioned early on in this book, my biggest fear in moving was being unable to replicate Richmond's warmth and beauty in Georgia. I had so many precious memories in my hometown, more than forty-five years of special moments and unique people. What if I couldn't find the same in my new home? Even after I decided to take the plunge and make the move, this fear remained. If anything, it grew as I planned a backyard barbecue for all my acquaintances, business friends, and frenemies.

I recommend to my clients that they find a one-stop way to say goodbye to people who are not close friends but still part of your life. It's better than organizing fifty private goodbyes to people who are important to you. It helped in my case that socially distanced outdoor events were among the few relatively safe activities.

It was a fun afternoon, bittersweet in the way that goodbyes often are. My heart was filled with love for all these people who had enriched my life in different ways over the years. Several people at the barbecue asked me if we could meet up again one-on-one before I left. I was touched, but I held firm on a piece of advice I give to my clients: Don't overcommit to social engagements in the final days prior to your move. If you are a people-pleaser like me, it's tempting to agree (or offer) to see as many people as often as you can, since you might not see them again or at least for a while. But doing so only adds to the pressure. Time will feel limited as the moving date gets closer—trust me on that. Stick to your guns and resist the urge to pack as many last-minute social events into your calendar as possible. For my kids, it was different—they had fewer people to say goodbye to, so I encouraged them to spend as much time with their friends as they could in our final weeks.

For closer friends and family members, I arranged lunches, dinners, and a few beer summits. I encouraged my kids to do the same (well, not the beer part). For one thing, our entire lives were in that town—trying to squeeze final meetings into the last week or weekend would be overwhelmingly emotionally and physically taxing. For another, it was important that we took the lead in front-loading the meetings, because in general, when you're moving, everyone will want to see you on your last day, unless you ensure otherwise.

Barbecue aside, I socialized outside my home mainly at other people's houses. I normally love cooking for others, but adding a bunch of food preparation and dirty dishes to wash on top of my moving responsibilities would add to the stress caused by the move. I recommend that my clients do the same. The goal is to be as stress-free as possible while you pack and get ready to move, since these proceedings are difficult enough. We went on our favorite hike, and to the best darn ice cream shop east of the Mississippi a few last times. If it seems sentimental, that's because it is. I always try to lean into the feelings rather than avoid them.

FEEL THE FEELINGS

Indeed, even with all my careful staggering of final meetings and goodbyes, leaving was still hard. Of course it was. Whatever my life would be in Georgia—and I wouldn't know for sure until I moved there—it would be different than it was in Richmond. Aunts, uncles, cousins, business associates, old friends, new friends—none would be a bike ride away any longer. I was surprised to find that I was growing nostalgic for not just people but places and things: the local pizza place, the park near my high school where I hung out with friends, and did I mention my favorite ice cream store, Gelati Celesti? It felt like my love of those places would somehow fade away into nothingness if I were not around them all the time.

But technology makes leaving a little easier. I made sure to add every last person I knew in Richmond as a friend on Facebook, and I connected with as many friends and neighbors on Instagram as I could. This acted as a balm on my emotions. Technology is actually making it easier to say "see you soon" instead of "goodbye forever."

TAKE PHOTOS OF THE HOUSE

In the final days before I moved, when the house was still packed with stuff, my kids and I went around with our phones and took snaps of our favorite spots in the home, the backyard, the front yard, and the view from my room. Then we went down the street taking shots of our neighbors' houses and the entire block. Once the moving truck drove away, we took pictures of the empty interior. We wanted to remember the place we loved as it was while we lived in it. And we wanted to remember the actual place itself, as it looked without us living there. We walked around telling our stories about each room. I especially loved talking about the den, where we'd enjoyed so many Christmases. One of my sons talked about jumping up and down on the bed in his bedroom, and the boys burst out laughing thinking about it—I hadn't known at the time and would have been furious, but now I just joined in the laughter. Months later, I'd recall us telling those stories about our home—creating new memories by talking about our old ones. That's the magic of storytelling. It was a reminder that our remembrances are not finite—we can always add more. I kept telling myself that throughout my final days in Richmond.

MOVING DAY

After more than a month of saying goodbye to my home and my hometown, I was ready to move. It felt right. My kids, however, had a harder time. I literally couldn't find my oldest son the morning we were leaving! I knew he hadn't gone missing—I wasn't worried about him ending up on a milk carton. But I'd noticed that the last few days had been tough on him, and I had expected moving day to be particularly difficult. I spent two hours looking for him on a day when I didn't have two hours to spare! Eventually I tracked him down—hiding in a closet with his best friend. He just didn't want to leave Richmond behind. I understood. Don't underestimate the emotional magnitude of moving; it can be deeply powerful. What matters is that you let those feelings into your life, so that they flow through you.

This incident is how I learned that it's best to keep any kids and pets away during the truck-packing. If you must have them with you, put them in a room away from the packing and label it so the movers don't go in and out. The goal is to keep it as stress-free for the kids and pets as possible, and to let the movers do their work. Once I found my eldest, the kids went with their mother so I could concentrate on moving.

Here is another tip for D-Day: Pack toiletries last in a box and put them at the back of the truck. You want toilet paper and soap immediately available for you and the movers, both as you're packing up and when you're unpacking. I recommend having bottles of water for the movers as well and some snacks like nuts and apples.

The other advice I have for moving day is to get out of the way if you've hired movers. Let them do their job. That's what you paid them to do. The last thing a professional needs is for you to tell them how to do their job. And remember: I broke my wrist checking up on them, and these were people I knew, had personally trained, and trusted!

BE OPEN TO LAST-MINUTE GLITCHES

The movers were loading up the truck when they got to some old sports equipment I'd had for decades: a kayak, a set of golf clubs, and a pair of snow skis. These were among the few objects I considered sacred enough to bring with us to Georgia. But as I watched the movers lift them, I had second thoughts. I hadn't used the clubs in five years, and I used the kayak and skis one time a year, at most. Could we do without them? I asked the movers to put them down while I reconsidered.

Here's something I recommend to clients: For rarely used items, consider decluttering and then renting if you ever need them. With today's on-demand economy, you can rent everything from lawn equipment to tools to paddleboards to generators. In a lot of cities, I see small local companies that rent these items by the day or hour. I asked the movers to pack up other boxes while I quickly looked online for rental companies in Georgia. Yes, I'd be able to rent skis, golf clubs, and kayaks—and newer models at that. So while the movers packed the truck,

I posted my last few items on Facebook Marketplace and sold them all for $150. Suddenly the moving truck was a little lighter and I would need to move a little less.

Ideally, I would have made this choice to sell earlier. But what's really important is that while it occurred in suboptimal order, my decision to get rid of stuff was the smart one. Decluttering, downsizing, and moving are complicated operations, and you should feel free to make last-minute changes. In fact, this can be a sign of growth, because you're getting into a new mindset. Just be sure when you make belated decisions that you're not going in the opposite direction—keeping stuff you already committed to getting rid of. And remember that it's nobody else's decision but your own.

UNPACKING

As soon as I stepped into my new home, I felt a sense of relief and even excitement. The moving truck hadn't arrived yet, but it was a beautiful modern farmhouse that my fiancée had designed and built. My sons started running around in the new space with her four kids, and I started to smile.

Here's how we unpacked, and how I unpack my clients: first, the bedrooms, making the beds and putting away our clothes. That was followed by the kitchen, and then the rest of the house. Your attic storage should be minimal, because hopefully you are using in your living spaces everything you brought. (Since we converted to minimalism, our attic is empty but for insulation.) Unpacking is a lot more fun than packing, always. You can do it faster, it's more exciting, and, most important, you start to see your new life materialize.

More unpacking tips:

- Allocate a specific space for your boxes as you unpack them. Break them down, ready for recycling or donating.
- If you're moving into a community that serves meals, ask the management to arrange to have dinner to make new friends!
- If the kids are old enough, have them set up their own rooms so they feel a sense of belonging and accomplishment, and then send them out to play and get used to the new place.

• • •

Six months after I moved in, I'm writing these words. Noticing our minimalist house, a new friend recently asked me, "What items did you leave behind?" To be honest, I don't even remember. I don't miss a single item I gave away or sold.

That's not saying it wasn't really hard to make the decision to move, and even harder to let go of some of the important items. You'll recall that at one point, I was so hesitant to let go that I almost gave up on the amazing life that I now have in a new state, with new friends and my incredible family. I almost gave it all up because I was scared. That last day in my old house was particularly difficult. It was the moment of truth, and all I could think and talk about was all the good times I'd had in Richmond. I was openly second-guessing my decision, talking with my kids about whether we were making the right move after all. Then my middle son looked me in the eye.

"We're just going to make new memories in our new home, Dad," he said, repeating the advice I've given my clients for the past twenty-plus years. "We're just leaving behind the stuff." I choked up and hugged him. He'd learned the lesson and was teaching it back to me.

Know this: Wherever you are going, you too can free your life of clutter and stuff. Shut the book and get started. A new, simpler, and better life awaits you when you do.

ACKNOWLEDGMENTS

I've been wanting to write this book for decades, but it took many people to make it a reality.

First, thanks to my dad, stepfather, grandmother, and both grandfathers. They're no longer with us, but the experiences of cleaning out their homes and learning their stories created the foundation of my career.

Thanks to my aunt BeBe for telling me incredible stories of our town while I cleaned out her house each summer.

Thanks to all my clients and their families for allowing me into your lives and trusting me to tell your stories and preserve your legacies. Without you and your trust, none of this would be possible.

Thank you to all my viewers, followers, and friends in the weird, wild world of social media and television. Your interest, interaction, and humor have inspired me to keep going and write this book.

To Jordan Michael Smith, my coauthor and friend, thank you for taking my crazy ideas and stories and crafting them into a thoughtful, positive, and entertaining book that I hope will help all who read it. You are a true wordsmith.

I'm blessed to have many professional partners who trust and support me no matter how wild my ideas are.

To my entire team at *Legacy List with Matt Paxton*, I am forever grateful. Avi, Mike, Lex, and Jaime, your friendship, expertise, and commitment are electric, and it shows on every episode that we create. Thank you for your time and devotion to making a show about longevity and legacy. To Michael Yudin, Joe Townley, and the entire MY Entertainment team: Thanks for hitting the road with me and helping us tell the incredible stories of our clients and their family legacies. Thanks to American Public Television, PBS, and, most important, Virginia Public Media. I can't give enough thanks to Jayme Swain, Steve Humble, and our listeners and supporters at VPM for allowing us to make the great show that is *Legacy List with Matt Paxton*. And thanks to my business partner and best friend, Neil Patel, my brother from another mother.

Thanks to my literary agent, Jane Dystel, at Dystel, Goderich & Bourret. You have been answering my calls and keeping me focused for over a decade. Thanks to my editor, Helen Healey, at Penguin Random House, who has the vision and foresight to publish a book about something everyone needs but nobody wants to talk about. Also thanks to copy editor Roland Ottewell and to Jen Huer, who designed our compelling cover. I also send my gratitude to AARP and particularly Jodi Lipson for partnering on this book. You are an amazing editor and quietly hilarious friend.

Finally, thanks to my mom and all the amazing women who raised me. Mom, you showed up every day and helped me through decades of growth. Through your actions, you taught me how to become a loving and compassionate person and the best parent I can be. You taught me to serve God, my community, and myself, in that order. Thank you for believing in me, supporting me, and finally acknowledging that this is a "real job." I love you more than I could ever tell you. Thanks to the city of Richmond, Virginia. God, I miss you like I miss a dear friend.

Finally, thanks to my wife, Zoë Kim, and our children, from the eldest (so no arguing!): Bella, Max, Cooper, Judd, Micah, Temple, and Marcus. You are everything that matters in my world. Thanks for the loud, crazy life that we are creating together. This family of nine is what inspired me to pack up our life and move. Change is scary, but you made surviving it worth every second. Thank you all for supporting my career and my heart. For a minimalist family of nine, we sure have everything.

RESOURCES

THROUGHOUT MY DECADES IN THE decluttering and downsizing business, I've relied on hundreds of trusted professionals and companies to help me get my work done. Now I'm sharing all my contacts with you. I try to give several options in each category. Use this as a starting point for your own research into local resources.

The first section answers the questions people asked me all the time: "What should I do with [fill in the blank]." The second section lists products and service companies I've used throughout my career that you might find helpful.

Items and resources are in alphabetical order. Disclaimer: A listing here does not imply an endorsement.

The information was current at the time we went to press in late 2021 but may now be outdated. **Find an updated version at my website, www.mylegacylist.com.**

DONATING, SELLING, RECYCLING, AND DISPOSING OF ITEMS

For a complete list of resources, see Products and Services, below.

ITEM	ACTION	RESOURCES AND ADVICE
Antiques (furniture and other Items)	Donate or sell	**Donate:** Buy Nothing groups on Facebook (www.facebook.com) Freecycle (www.freecycle.org) Goodwill (www.goodwill.org) Green Drop (www.greendrop.com) Habitat for Humanity ReStores (www.habitat.org/restores) Nextdoor (www.nextdoor.com) Salvation Army (www.salvationarmyusa.org) Thrift/resales stores Leave on the curb with a "FREE" sign on it (where local regulations allow) **Sell:** Antique stores Auction houses (see below and Step Eight) Facebook Marketplace (www.facebook.com/marketplace) 1stDibs (www.1stdibs.com) eBay (www.ebay.com) Etsy (www.etsy.com/sell) Ruby Lane (www.rubylane.com) Sotheby's (www.sothebys.com)

ITEM	ACTION	RESOURCES AND ADVICE
Appliances	Sell, recycle, or trash	**Sell:** Craigslist (www.craigslist.org) eBay (www.ebay.com) Facebook Marketplace (www.facebook.com/marketplace) Scrap metal shops (search online) **Recycle:** Contact your local waste services company to see if it offers appliance recycling services or can point you in the direction of government programs that recycle. **Trash:** If you're purchasing a new appliance, stores like Best Buy and Sears will haul away your old appliance for a fee when they deliver your new one.
Ashes	Discard	Check your state laws or local funeral home for any restrictions on scattering ashes. You can scatter them where the deceased asked you to, or, if no instructions were left, where you'd want to remember your loved one.
Autographed Items	Sell	Autographia (www.autographia.com) Heritage Auctions (www.ha.com)
Beanie Babies	Donate, sell, or trash	Conduct an internet search to see if your Beanie Babies are valuable; most aren't. For those that aren't: If they're unused, donate them to a local thrift store or charity that takes stuffed animals. If they're used, throw them away.

ITEM	ACTION	RESOURCES AND ADVICE
Books	Donate, sell, or recycle	**Donate:**
		Better World Books (www.betterworldbooks.com)
		BookMooch (www.bookmooch.com)
		Books for Soldiers (www.booksforsoldiers.com)
		Books Through Bars (www.booksthroughbars.org)
		Kids Need to Read (www.kidsneedtoread.org)
		Libraries
		Little Free Library (small boxes found in neighborhoods) (www.littlefreelibrary.org)
		Prison Book Program (www.prisonbookprogram.org)
		Reader to Reader (www.readertoreader.org)
		Retirement homes
		Schools
		Theaters (to use as props/displays)
		Sell:
		Bookstores (some may pay by the pound)
		Craigslist (www.craigslist.org)
		Facebook Marketplace (www.facebook.com/marketplace)

ITEM	ACTION	RESOURCES AND ADVICE
		Recycle: Paperback books can be placed in your curbside recycling bin. You may need to remove the covers from hardcover books before they can be recycled; check with your recycler.
Cars	Donate or sell	**Donate:** 1-800-Charity-Cars (www.800charitycars.org) Charitable Adult Rides & Services (where you can donate to a range of charities) (www.careasy.org) Vietnam Veterans of America Car Donation Program (www.vietnamveteranscardonation.org) **Sell:** CarLotz (www.carlotz.com) Carmax (www.carmax.com) Carvana (www.carvana.com) Search the internet for "Sell my car easy" to find local and national websites that will help you sell your car. Check reviews and Better Business Bureau ratings before choosing a company.
Compact discs, DVDs, vinyl records, eight-track tapes, cassette tapes	Donate, sell, or recycle	**Donate:** Thrift/resale stores **Sell:** Decluttr (www.decluttr.com) Discogs (a marketplace for old music, or, if you're not yet ready to sell, to catalog your collection) (www.discogs.com)

ITEM	ACTION	RESOURCES AND ADVICE
		EagleSaver (www.eaglesaver.com)
		eBay (www.ebay.com)
		Etsy (www.etsy.com)
		Sell DVDs Online (www.selldvdsonline.com)
		Used bookstores
		Recycle:
		CD Recycling Center of America (www .cdrecyclingcenter.org)
		GreenDisk (www.greendisk .com)
		Recycling bin or special drop-off areas (ask your recycler)
		Earth911 (https://search.earth911.com/)
China	Donate, sell, or "upcycle" (repurpose)	**Donate:**
		Art co-op
		Kids' art studio or camp
		Sell:
		Replacements.com (contact first to see if it can take your pattern) (www.replacements.com/sell -to-us)
		Upcycle:
		The Brooklyn Teacup (one of my favorite upcycling websites) (www.thebrooklynteacup.com)

ITEM	ACTION	RESOURCES AND ADVICE
Christmas decorations	Donate or sell	**Donate:** Buy Nothing groups on Facebook (www.facebook.com) Craigslist free section (www.craigslist.org) Freecycle (www.freecycle.org) Nextdoor (www.nextdoor.com) **Sell:** Craigslist (www.craigslist.org) Facebook Marketplace (www.facebook.com/marketplace)
Clothing	Donate, sell, or recycle	**Donate:** Dress for Success (professional clothing) (www.dressforsuccess.org) Free the Girls (bras) (www.freethegirls.org) Goodwill (www.goodwill.org) Green Drop (www.greendrop.com) Salvation Army (www.salvationarmyusa.org) Soles4Souls (shoes) (www.soles4souls.org) Thrift/resale stores **Sell:** ASOS Marketplace (http://marketplace.asos.com) Consignment shops (research first because some of these shops are great and others are not—see Step Seven)

ITEM	ACTION	RESOURCES AND ADVICE
		Depop (www.depop.com)
		Facebook Marketplace (www.facebook.com/ marketplace)
		Poshmark (I've sold a lot of nicer clothes through this app) (www.poshmark.com)
		ThredUp (www.thredup.com)
		Uptown Cheapskate (www.uptowncheapskate.com)
		Recycle:
		TerraCycle recycling boxes (www.terracycle.com)
		The North Face recycling program (takes any brand) (www.thenorthface.com)
Coins	Sell	The value of coins varies widely by quality and region.
		Coin shop
		Jeweler
		Pawnbroker (look for one who specializes in coins)
Comic books	Valuing and trading	**Valuing (and grading):**
		Certified Guaranty Company (www.cgccomics.com)
		Trading:
		1. Comic book store
		2. GoCollect (puts you in touch with respected buyers and sellers in the industry) (http://comics .gocollect.com)

ITEM	ACTION	RESOURCES AND ADVICE
Concert/rock posters and memorabilia	Sell	ASOS Marketplace (clothes) (http://marketplace.asos.com) Depop (clothes) (www.depop.com) eBay (www.ebay.com) Etsy (www.etsy.com) Facebook Marketplace (www.facebook.com/marketplace) Poshmark (clothes) (www.poshmark.com)
Crystal	Sell	You can identify crystal by holding the piece up to light. If you see a rainbow, it's genuine. Facebook Marketplace (www.facebook.com/marketplace) Replacements.com (www.replacements.com/sell-to-us)
David Winter Cottages	Sell	For best results, sell just before the holiday season and sell as a set, as opposed to individual pieces. Antique stores Craigslist (www.craigslist.org) eBay (www.ebay.com) Etsy (www.etsy.com) Facebook Marketplace (www.facebook.com/marketplace) Resale shop

ITEM	ACTION	RESOURCES AND ADVICE
Depression glass	Donate or sell	The market is poor because a lot of Depression glass is for sale. **Donate:** Thrift/resale stores **Sell:** DepressionGlassforSale.com (www.depressionglassforsale.com) Facebook Marketplace (www.facebook.com/marketplace) Replacements.com (www.replacements.com/sell-to-us)
Electronics (printers, photocopiers, VCR players, computer monitors, etc.)	Donate or recycle	**Donate:** World Computer Exchange (www.worldcomputerexchange.org) **Recycle:** Best Buy (www.bestbuy.com/recycle) Call2Recycle (rechargeable batteries and cell phones) (www.call2recycle.org) Computer Technology Association's Recycle Locator (https://www.cta.tech/Landing-Pages/Greener-Gadgets/Recycle-Locator#/) Office Depot (www.officedepot.com) Recycling center (https://search.earth911.com) Sprint's Buyback Program (www.sprintbuyback.com) Staples (www.staples.com/recycle)

ITEM	ACTION	RESOURCES AND ADVICE
Exercise equipment	Sell	Set expectations very low on pricing for this exercise equipment; you aren't the only person who bought this equipment and never used it, or stopped using it. Craigslist (www.craigslist.org) Facebook Marketplace (www.facebook.com /marketplace)
Food	Donate	Food banks (call to see what they accept and the best time for drop-off) Move for Hunger (www.moveforhunger.org)
Fur coats	Donate or sell	**Donate:** Coats for Cubs (donations help the rehabilitation of injured and orphaned animals across the United States; it was not operating at press time but did provide a list of places to independently donate to) (www.coatsforcubs.org) **Sell:** Depending on the type of fur, you may be unable to sell it. Some stores recommend getting fur appraised before selling. BuyMyFur (www.buymyfur .com) Cash for Fur Coats (www.cashforfurcoats.com) eBay (www.ebay.com)

ITEM	ACTION	RESOURCES AND ADVICE
Furniture	Donate or sell	**Donate:** Buy Nothing groups on Facebook (www.facebook.com) Craigslist free section (www.Craigslist.org) Freecycle Network (www.freecycle.org) Goodwill (www.goodwill.org) Green Drop (www.GreenDrop.com) Habitat for Humanity ReStores (www.habitat.org/restores) Leave on the curb with a "FREE" sign on it (where local regulations allow) Nextdoor (www.Nextdoor.com) Salvation Army (www.salvationarmyusa.org) Thrift/resale stores **Sell:** Facebook Marketplace (www.facebook.com/marketplace) Craigslist (Craigslist.org)
Glassware	Sell	**Sell:** Antique stores Craigslist (www.craigslist.org) eBay (www.ebay.com) Etsy (www.etsy.com) Facebook Marketplace (www.facebook.com/marketplace) Replacements.com (www.replacements.com/sell-to-us) Resale stores

ITEM	ACTION	RESOURCES AND ADVICE
Greeting cards	Donate	I recommend digitizing the important ones and recycling or throwing them all away, but if you want to donate them, try these places: Art school Kids' camp
Guns and ammunition	Surrender or sell	**Surrender:** Call the police, using a non-emergency line, who will walk you through the process of surrendering a firearm or connect you with a professional gun handler. **Sell:** Auction houses that specialize in guns (they may be able to legally pick up, transport, and sell the guns for you) Gun shops (they may offer you an in-home pickup price)
Historical items	Donate	History department of your local university or college Museum Veterans' group
Important papers	Shred	You can shred by hand or purchase a personal shredder, or use one of these: FedEx (www.fedex.com) Iron Mountain (large volume) (www.ironmountain.com) Recycling centers Shred-it (large volume) (www.shredit.com) UPS (www.theupsstore.com)

ITEM	ACTION	RESOURCES AND ADVICE
Ivory	Donate or sell	In most states and some countries, ivory (including pianos with ivory keys) cannot be sold. You'll need to know where and when the item was purchased or acquired. There are a few exceptions, so knowing the country of origin and year will help.
Jewelry	Appraise or sell	**Appraise:** American Society of Appraisers (www.appraisers.org/find -an-appraiser) International Society of Appraisers (www.isa-appraisers .org/find-an-appraiser) National Association of Jewelry Appraisers (www.najaappraisers.com /html/find_an_appraiser.php) **Sell:** Jeweler approved by the American Gem Society (www.american gemsociety.org)
Legos	Sell	BrickLink (specialty and rare Legos) (www.bricklink.com) Decluttr (www.decluttr.com /sell-lego) eBay (www.ebay.com) Facebook Marketplace (www.facebook.com /marketplace) StockX (www.stockx.com/lego)

ITEM	ACTION	RESOURCES AND ADVICE
License plates	Surrender, donate, or sell	**Surrender:** Local department of motor vehicles (which may require surrender of your plates) **Donate:** Art center **Sell:** There are collectable markets for some license plates, such as Delaware plates with low numbers. Research the internet for your specific plate value and your state laws regarding selling plates.
Lladró porcelain	Donate or sell	**Donate:** Buy Nothing groups on Facebook (www.facebook.com) Craigslist (www.craigslist.org) Freecycle (www.freecycle.org) **Sell:** Unfortunately, most Lladró figurines are not as valuable as they once were, but they are still collectable. Do your research first. eBay (www.ebay.com) Etsy (www.etsy.com) Facebook Marketplace (www.facebook.com /marketplace)
Military awards, memorabilia, and flags	Donate or dispose of	Flags should be donated to the Boy Scouts, Girl Scouts, or veterans groups, which have a specific way to properly dispose of them. For other items, contact the specific unit or local veteran group.

ITEM	ACTION	RESOURCES AND ADVICE
Model trains	Donate or sell	**Donate:** Buy Nothing groups on Facebook (www.Facebook.com) Craigslist (www.craigslist.org) Freecycle (www.freecycle.org) Thrift/resale stores (Goodwill, Salvation Army, etc.) **Sell:** eBay (www.ebay.com) Model railway trade shows and events ModelTrainMarket.com (www.modeltrainmarket.com/pages/sell-your-trains) SellMyTrains.com (www.sellmytrains.com) TrainMasterModels.com (www.trainmastermodels.com) Trainz.com (www.trainz.com/pages/sell-your-train)
Photos (old and historic)	Sell	Some old photos, including slides, can be sold, but you must know who owns them. U.S. copyright law gives creators ownership of the photo for life plus fifty years after their death. Art galleries Auction houses (listed in Products and Services below) eBay (www.ebay.com) Etsy (www.etsy.com)
Piano	Donate, sell, or dispose of	**Donate:** Beethoven Foundation (it won't accept every piano, but if it does accept yours, it will pick it up and give you a tax donation receipt) (www.beethovenfoundation.com)

ITEM	ACTION	RESOURCES AND ADVICE
		Buy Nothing groups on Facebook (state clearly in the listing that the buyer is responsible for all shipping/transportation) (www.facebook.com)
		Craigslist (state clearly in the listing that the buyer is responsible for all shipping/transportation) (www.craigslist.org)
		House of worship
		Pianos for Education (it won't accept every piano, but if it does accept yours, it will pick it up and give you a tax donation receipt; the proceeds go to music education.) (www.pianosforeducation.org)
		Schools and preschools
		Sell:
		Craigslist (www.craigslist.org)
		Piano shops (ask if they will sell your piano on consignment)
		Facebook Marketplace (www.facebook.com/marketplace)
		Trash:
		If you can't sell it or find a place to donate it, estimate that it will cost $200 to $300 to have a trash or junk company come to your house and remove the piano.
Postcards	Sell	Auction house
		eBay (www.ebay.com)
		Etsy (www.etsy.com)
		Flea markets
		Vintage stores

ITEM	ACTION	RESOURCES AND ADVICE
Prescription drugs	Discard	Chemicals and toxins from drugs that are disposed of into landfills or down toilets and sinks can escape into the ground and groundwater, polluting the environment and posing health hazards to humans, plants, and wildlife. Pills that are put in the trash can be easily removed from the garbage by people seeking to illegally use or sell them. Medications thrown in the trash can also be found and consumed by children or animals. To dispose of properly, follow the FDA guidelines at www.fda.gov/drugs/safe-disposal-medicines/disposal-unused-medicines-what-you-should-know **Among those guidelines:** Find a list of flushable drugs at www.fda.gov/drugs/disposal-unused-medicines-what-you-should-know/drug-disposal-fdas-flush-list-certain-medicines#FlushList Find drop-off locations at www.fda.gov/drugs/disposal-unused-medicines-what-you-should-know/drug-disposal-drug-take-back-locations Find a DEA-authorized collector in your area. (apps2.deadiversion.usdoj.gov/pubdispsearch/spring/main?execution=e1s1) Contact your local police or fire department for special drop-off days. Remove labels before recycling empty pill bottles.

ITEM	ACTION	RESOURCES AND ADVICE
Religious books	Donate	Donate religious books to a local house of worship. Many religious groups bury holy books out of respect.
Silver	Donate or sell	**Donate:** Buy Nothing groups on Facebook (www.facebook.com) **Sell:** Craigslist (www.craigslist.org) eBay (www.ebay.com) Facebook Marketplace (www.facebook.com /marketplace) Jewelry store (may pay you to melt it) Replacements.com (www.replacements.com)
Sneakers	Donate or sell	**Donate:** Buy Nothing groups on Facebook (www.facebook.com) Craigslist (www.craigslist.org) Freecycle (www.freecycle.org) Thrift/resale stores **Sell:** Flight Club (www.flightclub.com) Grailed (www.grailed.com /shop/sneakers) StockX (www.stockx.com)
Sports collectables	Sell	Autographia (www.autographia.com) Heritage Auctions (www.ha.com) SportsMemorabilia.com (www.sportsmemorabilia.com)

ITEM	ACTION	RESOURCES AND ADVICE
Stamps	Appraise and sell	**Appraise:** American Philatelic Society Dealer (www.stamps.org/dealers) Stamp collecting clubs (www.stamps.org/collect/clubs) Warwick & Warwick free valuations (www.warwickandwarwick.com) **Sell:** Auction sites eBay (www.ebay.com) Philatelic Traders Society (www.stamps.org) Stamp fairs (research the internet to find a local fair or convention)
Textbooks	Donate or sell	**Donate:** College library Local library **Sell:** BookFinder.com (search by ISBN to see offers; you don't pay shipping) (www.bookfinder.com) BookScouter (search by ISBN to see offers; this site works with forty-two buyback vendors) (www.bookscouter.com) College bookstores

ITEM	ACTION	RESOURCES AND ADVICE
Tools (hand or power)	Donate, sell, or recycle	**Donate:** Habitat for Humanity ReStores (www.habitat.org/restores /donate-goods) Thrift/resale stores **Sell:** Craigslist (www.craigslist.org) Facebook Marketplace (www .facebook.com/marketplace) **Recycle:** Recycling center (https://search .earth911.com)
Toys, stuffed animals, and games	Donate or recycle	**Donate:** Some places won't accept stuffed animals or items not in their original packaging. Elementary schools and preschools Goodwill (www.goodwill.org) Houses of worship Ronald McDonald House (www.rmhc.org) Salvation Army (www .salvationarmyusa.org) Shelters Toys for Tots (www.toysfortots.org) **Recycle:** Recycling center (https://search .earth911.com) TerraCycle Zero Waste Box (www .terracycle.com)

ITEM	ACTION	RESOURCES AND ADVICE
Trophies	Donate	Buy Nothing groups on Facebook (www.facebook.com) Craigslist (www.craigslist.org) Thrift shops (check first; I've found that many won't accept trophies)
Watches	Sell	Consult a local higher-end jewelry shop, not a national chain.
X-ray films	Discard	Contact a hospital or radiology clinic or a company such as www.xrayfilmsrecycling.com to find out how to discard of X-rays. They should be recycled, not put in the trash, since they won't break down in the landfill.
Yearbooks	Return to school or recycle	Consult the school to see if yearbooks can be returned there; if not, put them in your recycling bin.

PRODUCTS AND SERVICES

Appraisers

All these appraisers will charge a fee for their services.

American Society of Appraisers (www.appraisers.org /find-an-appraiser)

International Society of Appraisers (www.isa-appraisers .org/find-an-appraiser)

National Association of Jewelry Appraisers
  (www.najaappraisers.com/html/find_an_appraiser.php)

WorthPoint (lists how much items have sold for at
  auctions. This is a service and does charge a fee.)
  (www.worthpoint.com)

Auction Houses

Christie's (www.christies.com)

CT Bids (www.ctbids.com)

Everything But The House (www.ebth.com)

Heritage Auctions (www.ha.com)

MaxSold (www.maxsold.com)

National Auctioneers Association
  (www.auctioneers.org)

Sotheby's (www.sothebys.com)

Bio- or Medical Waste Disposal

Cantel Medical Waste (www.cantelmedical.com)

Clean Earth (www.cleanearthinc.com)

Stericycle (www.stericycle.com)

Carpet Cleaners

The best professional carpet cleaners tend to be local, so do your research to find some nearby companies that have great reviews. Here are a few national brands I have worked with:

ServiceMaster Restore (www.servicemasterrestore.com)
Servpro (www.servpro.com/carpet-upholstery-cleaning)
Stanley Steemer (www.stanleysteemer.com)

Charity Evaluator

Charity Navigator (www.charitynavigator.org)
Give.org (www.give.org)
GuideStar (www.guidestar.org)

Cleaning Supplies

Bathroom tile and grout cleaner

Dremel Versa (www.dremel.com)

Hardwood cleaners

Bissell (www.bissell.com)
Bona (www.bona.com)
Swiffer (www.swiffer.com)

Microfiber towels

Almost any retail store will have generic-branded microfiber towels that will do well. I use Norwex towels because they are long-lasting, but you will find many microfiber towels available at most retail stores.

Norwex (www.norwex.com)

Vacuums

Miele (www.mieleusa.com)
Oreck (www.oreck.com)
Simplicity (www.simplicityvac.com)

Cleaning Supplies

Amazon (www.amazon.com)
Home Depot (www.homedepot.com)
Lowe's (www.lowes.com)
Walmart (www.walmart.com)

Donation and Resale Centers

If you're going to try to take a tax deduction for your donations, ask for a receipt. Many of these places will pick up.

Goodwill (www.goodwill.org)
Green Drop (www.greendrop.com)

Habitat for Humanity ReStores
   (www.habitat.org/restores)
Salvation Army (www.salvationarmyusa.org)
Vietnam Veterans of America (www.vva.org/donate)

Donations Online

Buy Nothing Project (on Facebook or app) (www.facebook
   .com)
Craigslist free section (www.craigslist.org)
Freecycle Network (www.freecycle.org)
Nextdoor (website or app) (www.nextdoor.com)

Home Inventory Tracking

Full disclosure: I'm on FairSplit's board of advisors. Its service offers an online system to inventory and track items in a home.

FairSplit (www.fairsplit.com)

Junk and Trash Disposal

1-800-Got-Junk? (www.1800gotjunk.com)
College Hunks Hauling Junk & Moving

(www.collegehunkshaulingjunk.com)

Junk King (www.junk-king.com)

Mold Remediation/Mitigation Companies

First Onsite (www.firstonsite.com)

ServiceMaster Restore (www.servicemasterrestore.com)

Servpro (www.servpro.com)

Moving Companies

Bekins (www.bekins.com)

College Hunks Hauling Junk & Moving (www
.collegehunkshaulingjunk.com)

Wheaton World Wide Moving (www.wheaton
worldwide.com)

You Move Me (www.youmoveme.com)

Moving and Organizing Professionals

National Association of Productivity & Organizing
Professionals (www.napo.net)

National Association of Senior & Specialty Move
Managers (www.nasmm.org)

Moving Supplies

Amazon (www.amazon.com)

Home Depot (www.homedepot.com)

Lowe's (www.lowes.com)

Northern Tool & Equipment (www.northerntool.com)

Tractor Supply Company (www.tractorsupply.com)

U-Line (www.uline.com)

Walmart (www.walmart.com)

Paper Shredding (high volume)

Iron Mountain (www.ironmountain.com)

Shred-it (www.shredit.com)

UPS Store (www.theupsstore.com)

Photo Organization and Digitization

Legacybox (www.legacybox.com)

Memories by Matt Paxton
   (www.memoriesbymattpaxton.com)

Photomyne (www.photomyne.com)

The Photo Managers (www.thephotomanagers.com)

Photo Storage

Forever (www.forever.com)

Photomyne (www.photomyne.com)

SmugMug (www.smugmug.com)

Selling Online

Craigslist (www.craigslist.org)

eBay (www.ebay.com)

EstateSales.net (www.estatesales.net)

Facebook Marketplace (www.facebook
.com/marketplace)

Mercari (www.mercari.com)

OfferUp (www.offerup.com)

Poshmark (www.poshmark.com)

ThredUp (www.thredup.com)

Storage

CubeSmart (www.cubesmart.com)

Extra Space Storage (www.extraspace.com)

MakeSpace (www.makespace.com)

Public Storage (www.publicstorage.com)

U-Haul (www.uhaul.com/storage)

Thrift/Resale Stores

Goodwill (www.goodwill.org)

Salvation Army (www.thesalvationarmy.org)

Truck Rental

Enterprise (www.enterprisetrucks.com)

Hertz (www.hertz.com)

Penske (www.pensketruckrental.com)

U-Haul (www.uhaul.com)

Upcycling

The Brooklyn Teacup (www.thebrooklynteacup.com)

Upcycle That (www.upcyclethat.com)

Visit www.mylegacylist.com for an updated list of resources.

INDEX